Getting Skilled with Java

Learn Java Programming from Scratch with Realistic Applications and Problem Solving Programmes

M Rashid Raza

www.bpbonline.com

FIRST EDITION 2022

ISBN: 978-93-91392-499

LIMITS OF LIABILITY AND DISCLAIMER OF WARRANTY

www.bpbonline.com

Dedicated to

My beloved Parents

M Sarmad

Mazda Tabassum

&

My family and friends

About the Author

Mohammad Rashid Raza is a software developer with a wide range of interests in fields such as microservices, information theory, basic programming, systems and architecture, and distributed systems. He has worked on numerous projects in web application and software development fields as a full-stack developer in various domains like CGP, CMS, Education, Payments and Finance, Airlines, and Travel. He earned his Bachelor's Degree in Political Science from the University of Delhi, New Delhi and a Master's degree in Computer Applications from the Indira Gandhi National Open University, New Delhi. He has earned certifications from Adobe on Adobe Experience Manager developer and architect, from Microsoft on Microsoft .Net framework developer. He is a regular blogger (at **rashidjorvee@blogspot.com**) and is a computer programming education enthusiast.

About the Reviewers

- **Rati Mehra** is a Java architect with 12 years of extensive experience in Java technologies and designing web world solutions and architectures. Rati completed her Bachelor's degree in Technology from Amity University, Noida, and her Master's from Symbiosis, Pune.

- With nine years of experience in the IT industry, **Amritpal Singh** is an enthusiast in Full Stack Development. He is currently working for Larsen & Toubro Infotech as a Project Lead. His skills in Web Application, Backend Application, Middleware Application, Cloud and many more has seen him grow as a Java Full Stack Development expert. Amritpal Singh has earlier worked for top IT companies like HCL Technologies , Tech Mahindra , Cognizant Technologies and has contributed to top client projects such as American Airlines, USA Bank, Walmart, Nokia and Citibank. He has explored himself as a writer with his book Affinity. He is mentoring and playing a role of Interview Panelist for hiring new talent. Amrit is also a contributor on Stack Overflow. He now focuses on channeling his knowledge into open source projects and sharing with the community by mentoring, creating POCS, running workshops, writing blogs to help make the world a better and more developed place.

- **Neha Sehdev** has a Bachelor's Degree in Computer Applications from Guru Nanak Dev University and Master's in Computer Applications from Punjab Technical University. Neha has 8 years of teaching experience in Computer Science and programming and has a true passion to work with young learners. Neha likes to use her skills to help children progress in all areas of development. Apart from teaching, Neha is also passionate about writing articles and blogs and has also contributed to many primary school books. Neha enjoys reading, cooking, listening to music, spending time with friends and family and also watching horror stories.

Acknowledgement

There are a few people whom I want to thank for the continued and ongoing support they have given me during the writing of this book. First and foremost, I would like to thank my parents for all their effort and support and my friends who encouraged me to write this book.

I am grateful to my mentors who also helped me to learn and guided me to skill myself in Java programming and other computer and internet technologies. I am thankful for the excellent online release notes and Java docs provided by Oracle and Java bloggers to understand the product and new features in-depth.

My gratitude also goes to the team at BPB Publications for being supportive enough and providing me ample time to draft the book and guiding me throughout the publishing process. The whole team of BPB, including the technical reviewers (Amrit, Neha, and Rati) were instrumental in getting the book in much better shape than I could have ever managed.

Preface

This book covers the high-level computer programming language Java, starting from fundamentals of computer programming to advanced level of programming concepts using core Java programs. The key focus is on guiding a beginner or developer to learn Java programming from scratch and implement different classes, objects, and libraries of Java while writing the code. This book focuses on some of the most frequently used object-oriented design patterns and their implementation using Java.

The book describes the theoretical concepts of every module of Java, that is required to write a program and also the analytical part that helps to apply the right features of Java to convert the requirement into a Java program. The book also demonstrates the setup of the machine for Java development and the installation guide for the java software development kit, that is Java development kit (JDK). Every chapter has examples and sample programs that help to understand the concept with the actual implementation, followed by quite a few challenging questions, exercises, and problems to create an opportunity for the readers to test the skills they have learned.

This book starts with the introduction and history of programming in **chapter 1.** In this chapter, we will discuss the types of computer programming such as high-level and low-level programming. We will also explore the history of Java programming. We will learn about the JDK and its module that is required to run Java in our machine.

In **chapter 2,** we will study about the software required to run Java on the computer and how to prepare our machine to write and run a program in the Java language. We have provided step-by-step details for installing JDK and setting up the environment variable.

In **chapter 3,** we will discuss the foundation of high-level Java programming. We will learn to create a Java file and declare the classes and methods. We will also discuss the use of packages and access specifiers along with the creation of variables in Java using various data types.

In **chapter 4,** we will discuss the types of constructors and how to create a constructor. We will also understand the use of constructors and their relation with parent and child class.

In **chapter 5,** we will learn about the static keyword and the use of static keywords with variables, objects, code blocks, and classes in Java. We will also learn in detail about the advantages of static keywords.

In **chapter 6,** we will learn to work on String objects and String data types and use different types of String classes and their methods to manipulate or control the String data.

In **chapter 7,** we will discuss how to manage the list of data or multiple values of the same data type using a single variable. Also, we will learn to create a fixed list of constant data. Here, we will talk about Array and Enum types of objects.

In **chapter 8,** we will learn decision-making skills, or how to set conditions before executing any statement and then based on the conditions, execute the set of statements in Java programming. Also, we will study iteration or looping to read and write the data from or into a list, or perform or run a block of code or statement multiple times, again based on condition.

In **chapter 9,** we will study casting and wrapping variables into classes using wrapper classes, and also learn how to make the code type-safe using generics to avoid run time errors in the program.

In **chapter 10,** we will study about the main feature of programming that is object-oriented programming which helps a developer to choose the right approach of programming while designing the solution. Here, we will learn all the approaches of OOPs programming using Encapsulation, abstraction, inheritance, and polymorphism.

In **chapter 11,** we will study how to handle runtime errors in our program and application. This is a very important feature that a developer should follow to keep the application active even after receiving incorrect or bad data or information. Handling exceptions and errors help us to handle the situations of invalid and bad data or object and also helps to perform some additional activities to move the flow of the program in a different direction.

In **chapter 12,** we will learn how to manage a group of data in Java Collection. This is an advanced feature of Java programming that we use to handle a group of data and manipulate the data using various Java collection classes and interfaces. Also, we will discuss the collections class and its method that help write the program.

In **chapter 13,** we will read about serialization and deserialization, that is, storing data into a file and reading data from a file. Here, we will learn about different classes and approaches to read and write and handle different types of files (for example, JSON, XML, TXT, XLS, CSV).

In **chapter 14,** we will learn how we can utilize the CPU and execute multiple programs simultaneously or execute the same program in chunks by splitting the parts of the program into the smallest execution units using Thread. We will also practice the creation of Thread and how to split and run our program in chunks.

In **chapter 15,** we will see how we can create a bridge between our Java program or application and database (SQL or NoSQL). We will learn how to establish connectivity with any database management system and get and set data from Java applications. We will discuss various libraries and classes that are being used to perform all these in Java.

In **chapter 16,** we will take a deep dive into Java managing memory and see how Java manages the memory of our machine. Java has an inbuilt feature which is called garbage collection to take care of the memory which is responsible for allocation and deallocation of memory of Java objects and keeping our program or application active without any memory leakage.

Code Bundle and Coloured Images

Please follow the link to download the
Code Bundle and the *Coloured Images* of the book:

https://rebrand.ly/034fe8

The code bundle for the book is also hosted on GitHub at **https://github.com/bpbpublications/Getting-Skilled-with-Java**. In case there's an update to the code, it will be updated on the existing GitHub repository.

We have code bundles from our rich catalogue of books and videos available at **https://github.com/bpbpublications**. Check them out!

Errata

We take immense pride in our work at BPB Publications and follow best practices to ensure the accuracy of our content to provide with an indulging reading experience to our subscribers. Our readers are our mirrors, and we use their inputs to reflect and improve upon human errors, if any, that may have occurred during the publishing processes involved. To let us maintain the quality and help us reach out to any readers who might be having difficulties due to any unforeseen errors, please write to us at :

errata@bpbonline.com

Your support, suggestions and feedbacks are highly appreciated by the BPB Publications' Family.

Piracy

If you come across any illegal copies of our works in any form on the internet, we would be grateful if you would provide us with the location address or website name. Please contact us at **business@bpbonline.com** with a link to the material.

If you are interested in becoming an author

If there is a topic that you have expertise in, and you are interested in either writing or contributing to a book, please visit **www.bpbonline.com**. We have worked with thousands of developers and tech professionals, just like you, to help them share their insights with the global tech community. You can make a general application, apply for a specific hot topic that we are recruiting an author for, or submit your own idea.

Reviews

Please leave a review. Once you have read and used this book, why not leave a review on the site that you purchased it from? Potential readers can then see and use your unbiased opinion to make purchase decisions. We at BPB can understand what you think about our products, and our authors can see your feedback on their book. Thank you!

For more information about BPB, please visit **www.bpbonline.com**.

Table of Contents

Chapter 1
Introduction to Java

You have opted for one of the most prominent and advanced programming languages to get skilled in. Our curriculum is easy to understand and best for any beginner and developer to get expertise in Java programming. Let's begin our journey towards Java.

Every time when we heard about a new thing or term, the initial questions that comes in our mind are: "What is this?", "Why is this?", "What people do with this?" This is the nature of a human being and his/her curiosity to get to know about new things. People generally approach someone nearby to get to know more about new terms. Today, we live in the world of Internet. Hence, all our questions hit the search engine; either Google, Bing, or Yahoo.

When we intend to learn something new, we have to start from its base and foundation. In this chapter, we will discuss the foundation of the computer programming language and how computer programming get enhanced day by day to fulfil the human needs. We will also discuss the foundation of Java language, how Java works, and what all we require to design, write, and run a Java program.

Structure

In this chapter, we will discuss the following topics:

- Java programming

- History of computer programming
- Why developers prefer to write in Java
- Software development kit (SDK)
- Java development kit (JDK)
- Java virtual machine (JVM)

Objectives

After successfully completion of this chapter, you will be able to:

- Discuss and explain the history of computer programming and the need for it
- Discuss the various computer programming languages
- Understand the Java programming language
- Understand why Java programming is widely used by programmers
- Explain the various types of programming languages and their uses
- Explain the software development kit and Java development kit
- Discuss the mechanism of compiler, interpreter, and execution of program
- Explain the architecture of Java foundation

Introduction to Java

Java is a high-level, object-oriented, functional programming language used to develop and design the computer- or mobile-based application and software. The pattern of Java programming is based on C++, which is also an object-oriented programming language. Java was developed by computer scientist James Gosling and his team in year 1991 in the Sun Microsystems lab.

Types of programming languages

There are two types of programming languages that we use to perform some operation on a computer and machine.

Low-level language

The low-level language is directly understood by the computer processor. We can only interact with hardware using binary numbers, 0 and 1 since machine and processor understand only the binary number and need all inputs only in the binary format to perform the operation. We have two types of low-level languages:

- **The machine language**: The machine language is made up of binary numbers, in which we have every command written in the binary format. This language is very fast since there is no interpreter required to convey the command to the processor. The processor can easily understand the steps written in binary. The machine language is also known as **first generation language** (**1GL**).

  The following is a machine language program sample to add two numbers variables. This program is just to show you how a machine code looks like. Don't mess yourself into this:

Location Hex	Instruction Code Binary	Instruction Code Hex	Instruction	Comments
100	0010 0001 0000 0100	2104	LDA 104	Load first operand into AC
101	0001 0001 0000 0101	1105	ADD 105	Add second operand to AC
102	0011 0001 0000 0110	3106	STA 106	Store sum in location 106
103	0111 0000 0000 0001	7001	HLT	Halt computer
104	0000 0000 0101 0011	0053	operand	83 decimal
105	1111 1111 1111 1110	FFFE	operand	-2 decimal
106	0000 0000 0000 0000	0000	operand	Store sum here

Example 1.1: *A machine language program sample to add two numbers variables*

- **Assembly language**: Assembly language is also a low-level language, but provides some ease to humans to write the program and understand what they will command to the processor to perform. Instead of binary numbers (that is, 0 or 1), we use the symbolic operation code to write the statement, that is, add, sub, mov.

  With the help of assembler, the assembly language program is compiled and converted into the machine language in string of 0 and 1 to get executed by processor. The assembly language is also known as **second generation language** (**2GL**).

  The following is an example of the assembly language program to add two numbers. This program is just to show you how an assembly program looks like. Don't mess yourself into this:

```
data segment
a db 09h
b db 02h
c dw ?
data ends

code segment
assume cs:code,ds:data
start:
mov ax,data
mov ds,ax
mov al,a
mov bl,b
add al,bl
mov c,ax
int 3
code ends
end start
```

***Example 1.2**: An example of assembly language program to add two numbers*

The preceding program is just for your reference so that you can visualize how an assembly program looks like.

High-level language

The high-level language is also known as **third generation language** (**3GL**). The high-level language consists of the statement and syntax. These syntaxes are meaningful, and a person can easily learn and understand the programs. Execution of the program follows the order of the steps written in the program and executed one by one to reach the desired result.

Java is an example of a high-level programming language. While writing a Java program, we keep the result in mind and then write the steps to get the desired result from that program just like an algorithm. C, C++, COBOL, and FORTAN are examples of **high-level programming language** (**HLL**).

```
public class AddTwoNumbers {
  public static void main(String[] args) {
    int a = 5, b = 6, result;
    result = a + b;
```

```
    System.out.println("Addition of two numbers is: " +result);
  }
}
```

***Example 1.3**: An example of a high-level program to add two numbers using Java*

The preceding program is written in Java to add two numbers and print the result as an output on the console. In the upcoming chapters, we will discuss every syntax of this programming one by one.

History of computer programming

The very first programming language was developed during the time of invention of computer by Ada Lovelace for Charles Babbage. After that, there is a huge list of programming languages developed by computer scientists and engineers for different purposes and needs. We will discuss few programming languages in this chapter, their invention, who invented and when:

- **Algorithm for analytical engine**: In the year 1883, a mathematician and colleague of Charles Babbage wrote an algorithm to compute the Bernoulli number (a sequence of rational number).
- **Assembly language**: In the year 1949, Kathleen Booth created a new language to interact with the computer. This is a low-level language to simplify the language of machine of code, so that a human would not struggle and mess with 0 and 1 to deal with computer. It was almost written as a machine code with operands and instructions, but in an understandable string.
- **Autocode**: The first Autocode and its compiler was developed by a British computer scientist Alick Edwards Glennie for Mark1 computer at University of Manchester. Autocode is the first programming language where compiler used to compile the program written in Autocode.
- **Formula Translation (Fortran)**: In the year 1957, John Backus developed a language to simplify the computation of scientific, numerical, statistical, and mathematical calculations, which we called Fortran.
- **COBOL**: COBOL stands for **common business-oriented language**. In the year 1959, an American computer scientist Grace Brewster Murray Hopper developed this language for business use. The best part of this language is that the syntax that we write the program in is written in the English language. COBOL is still used in many domains, which we use in our daily life like mainframe, banking, traffic signaling, and so on.
- **BASIC**: In the year 1964, the mathematician John Kemeny and Thomas Kurtz developed a non-structured and general-purpose computer programming

language to make the computer accessible for non-technical students as well. The motto of this development was to involve everyone towards the computer, even for those who did not know the technical and scientific things, because before this people had to write their own software or program to use the computer. BASIC stands for beginner's all-purpose symbolic instruction code.

- C: In the year 1972, an American computer scientist, Dennis Ritchie at Bell Labs developed C programming. This is based on BCPL (basic combined programming language). This is considered as a first high-level program language and widely used to interact with hardware. The C programming has been standardized by ANSI and ISO since 1989. This is being used for operating system applications, super computers, and embedded systems.

- C++: C was upgraded to C++ in 1985 by Bjarne Stroustrup. This is class-based, object-oriented, general-purpose programming language, and used in high-performance software and applications.

- **Python**: In the year 1991, Python was developed by Guido Van Rossum. Python is an object-oriented, easy, and efficient programming language for data science programs. Using Python, we must write very few lines of codes, to the point and only logical codes to get the expected result.

- **Visual Basic**: In the year 1991, this was developed by Microsoft corporation. This was the first programming language in computer history, in which the developer could reuse the existing module of code as a component. For that, visual basic provided a rich **graphical user interface** (**GUI**) to simply drag-and-drop the reusable components to add the functionality of that code in their new application and software.

- **Java**: In the year 1995, Java was developed by James Gosling in Sun Microsystems. Java is a class-based, object-oriented, functional programming, multi-purpose programming language. Java is well known for its best feature, which once complied, Java code can run on any operating system, which makes Java platform independent. The compiled code can run on any machine where JVM is installed. In September 2019, Java 13 has been released by Oracle.

- **C# (C sharp)**: In the year 2001, C# was launched by Microsoft. C# is also an object-oriented programming language and is developed on the same pattern as Java and C++ are developed. This language is being used in almost all Microsoft products.

- **GO**: In the year 2009, Google developed this programming language by focusing of current programming world. A program written in Go is a fast, statically typed, compiled language that feels like a dynamically typed, interpreted language. The syntax used in Go is like C.

Here, we have tried to list few of the most used programming languages by software developers. The list of programming languages is very long and ongoing. In this era of computer, every day we have a requirement, and to fulfil the requirement and gap, the computer scientists keep developing frameworks and languages.

Features of Java

Java has many unique features that are not available in other programming language. We will discuss the few outstanding features of Java that encourage developers to write their application and software using Java programming. Using Java, we can develop the complete application and software. Here are the features of Java programming language:

- **Platform independent**: Java is platform independent; it means we can build the code at once and then deploy and run in any machine or server.
- **Scalability**: Java is an object-oriented programming language, which makes the code modular, scalable, and easy to use and write.
- **Library**: Java has a very huge open-source library available in the market. Since it is open source and free program, anyone can contribute to create java library. These libraries later can be used by developers to write their code.
- **Development for all device**: It supports all kinds of development for all platforms. We can develop desktop, web, and mobile applications using Java.
- **Open source JDK**: Java is open source. A user can download the JDK from the official site and use it. A student or developer of Java need not pay anything to use Java. An individual developer or group of developers may contribute as well in JDK to build new classes and methods.
- **Easy**: Java is easy to learn and use. Many books and online materials are available to study Java language.
- **Development tool**: Some excellent IDEs are available for Java developers such as Eclipse, NetBeans, and IntelliJ. These tools have IntelliSense that keep providing hints to developers to complete the syntax and statement of code.

These features of Java make it popular among the developers to get trained and encourage them to write their programs using Java.

Software required to run Java

Every software comes with a software development kit. That software development kit consists of all the required libraries and packages, which we need to write, and build the code written by developers. To start working with Java, we need the **Java development Kit (JDK)** to be installed in our machine. JDK is freely available and can be downloaded from Java's official website. There are three modules of Java available in the market:

- **J2EE**: Java enterprise edition advance module of Java where we can use EJB, servlet, JNDI, and JMS. It also includes the J2SE. So, we can use the API and libraries of Java in our advance Java programming.
- **J2SE**: Java standard edition is SDK for core Java libraries and API that we mainly use to develop the application and program. This includes the API such as util and lang.
- **J2ME**: Java micro edition is the lightweight version of Java SDK. This is mainly used to develop the application and software for portable and small devices such as mobiles, tablets, and so on.

These three modules are for different purposes. You may start with standard edition where almost everything is available for a Java developer.

Java Development Kit

JDK is a software development kit that provides the complete development environment to write and execute a Java program. Every programming language has its own software development kit. It creates the development environment in your machine and makes the required libraries available for you. You may refer the JDK official document to know all the out of the box available Java API specifications.

JDK consists of JRE and JVM.

Role of JDK:

- JDK compiles the Java source code (`.java`) into bytecode (`.class`). The type bytecode later can be executed on the JRE to run the software and application. After compilation, JDK creates .class file for every JAVA file with the same name. For example, the **`example.class`** file is the compiled version of the `example.java` source file.
- JDK also helps us to debug the code. We can easily start the debugging option using modern IDEs and execute the program statement by statement.

Java runtime environment

Every Java-based program needs some set of libraries and components to run the application or program developed in Java. JRE makes those libraries and components available for your Java program, so that your program can resolve the required dependencies. Using the JRE, you can only run the application and program written in Java. You cannot write a new Java program and compile it using JRE. To do so, you need JDK.

Java virtual machine

Java Virtual Machine ensures the platform for Java program, where a program written in Java will execute. This makes your computer compatible to run a software and application compiled in Java. It interprets the compile code (`.class` file) and enables it to run.

Java is platform independent, which means it will compile at once and the same compile code will be compatible and can run on any operating system. Did you ever think how Java is able to manage all this and run on every operating system, but on other hand, no other programming languages are? This is all because of JVM. When you install JDK or JRE in your machine, Java creates its own virtual machine JVM in the **operating system** (**OS**) to run the program written in Java.

Just-in-time compiler (JIT)

The just-in-time compiler is a part of Java virtual machine and present wherever JVM is present. It helps the JVM to compile the bytecode (java .class file) received from JRE into machine code instructions. Since a machine and its hardware only understand the machine language, JIT helps JVM to convert those codes/programs into machine language so that it can be executed and operated by the machine.

The following *Figure 1.1* explains the complete architecture of Java development kit and its members that are a part of JDK. We have already discussed the various parts of JDK such as JRE, JVM and JIT, and their role in Java:

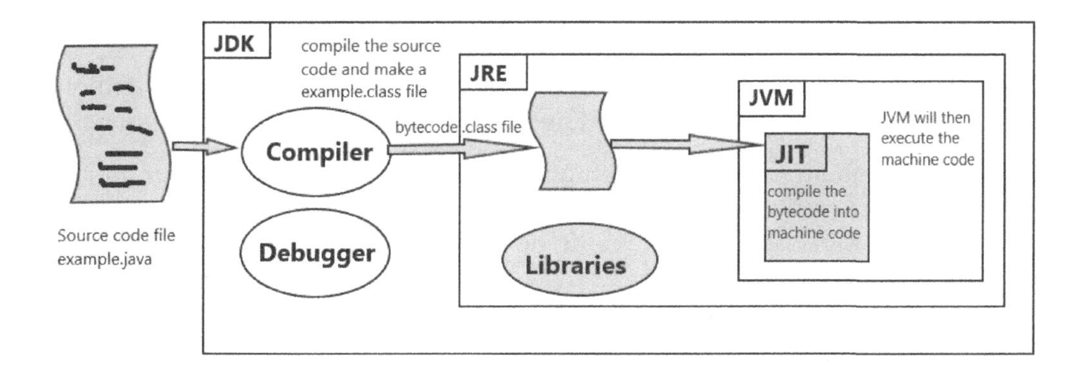

***Figure 1.1**: Java code compilation and execution process*

The *Figure 1.1* shows how a code written in Java/Java source code gets executed in the machine and through what steps it must pass to complete the successful execution to generate the result.

In the first step, example.java file gets compiled by JDK and converts the Java code into bytecode and save it into a new file **`example.class`**. Also, all syntax and compilation errors can be fixed at this moment only. If your code has any syntax error, the compiler will fail to compile your source file.

In the second step, JRE comes in picture and as an input, it takes the bytecode file created by JDK with the .class file extension. In our case, it is **`example.class`**. Now, JRE will resolve the bytecode with the required classes and objects and pass it to JVM to execute.

In the third step, JVM receives the **`example.class`** file. Since JVM doesn't understand the bytecode, it will send it to one of its member JIT, which will convert the bytecode into machine code so that JVM can understand and execute the code.

Conclusion

Java is a high-level computer programming language, which is used to design applications and software for any device. It is platform independent. A Java compiled code can run on any machine. JDK is the software development toolkit for Java, which consists of JRE and JVM. Java came to the market in the year 1995 and the latest version of Java is 13, which was released in September 2019.

A machine can only understand the program written in the machine language. It is very difficult to write a program for long calculations in machine language. Hence, we use high-level programming languages to write the program. These programs are later compiled and interpreted by the compiler and gets converted into bytecode and machine language.

Computer languages are categorized into three types, machine, assembly and high level. This is also known as the generation of computer programming language.

In this chapter, you have learned the foundation architecture of Java programming, the history of computer programming and its types. Hope you all have a clear picture in your mind about these. In the next chapter, we will learn how to set up our machine or computer for Java.

Points to remember

- The Java development kit (JDK) is required to write a Java program.
- Java is platform independent and can run on any operating system.

- Java creates its own virtual machine inside a machine to run the Java program when you install JRE and JDK in your machine.
- JRE, JVM, and JIT are part of JDK.

Multiple choice questions

1. **Which is responsible to interpret the bytecode into machine code?**
    a. Java virtual machine
    b. Java runtime environment
    c. Java compiler
    d. Just in time compiler
2. **In which year was Java developed?**
    a. 1987
    b. 1990
    c. 1995
    d. 1991
3. **Java runtime environment (JRE) consists of:**
    a. JDK and JVM
    b. JDK and JIT
    c. JDK, JRE and JVM
    d. JVM

Answers

1. **d**
2. **c**
3. **d**

Questions

1. What is JDK, JRE and JVM?
2. Why Java is platform independent?
3. Who invented Java programming and when?

Key terms

- **IntelliSence**: A feature for code completion, where user gets the hints what could be the next possible method and parameter to complete the statement of code. This is also known as auto complete or code assist.
- **Functional programming**: Functional programming is a term where we drag every statement of program into a mathematical function. We use operator, operands, functions and focus on solving a problem.
- **Object oriented programming**: This is a pattern of programming based on objects. It will consist of class and object based on real world system.
- **Compiler**: It converts or interprets program written in high level language into machine language (binary).

Glossary

- **ANSI**: American National Standards Institute
- **CLI**: Command line interface
- **GL**: Generation language
- **GUI**: Graphical user interface
- **HLL**: High level language
- **ISO**: International organization for standardization
- **JDK**: Java Development kit
- **JIT**: Just in time
- **JRE**: Java runtime environment
- **JVM**: Java virtual machine
- **OS**: Operating system
- **SDK**: Software development kit
- **IDE**: Integrated development environment

References

1. https://www.oracle.com/technetwork/java/javase/downloads/index.html
2. https://docs.oracle.com/en/java/javase/11/docs/api/index.html
3. https://docs.oracle.com/en/java/javase/13/books.html
4. https://en.wikipedia.org/wiki/History_of_programming_languages

CHAPTER 2
Installation Guide

To use any software and application, we need to install the software and application library files on the computer. In the same way, to start the development with any programming language, we must install the software development kit on our machine. The SDK contains the required programs and libraries for the software to run. Some of them are open source (free to use) and few are chargeable (we must pay to get the license to use the software).

In this chapter, we will learn how to prepare our machine for Java development. JDK is free for development and practice purpose. We have to get the paid license to use the same software in our production environment. Java development kit is a software development kit for Java. We will also see how to get the JDK and install on our computer. The environment variable is a system variable where we set the path of the directory where the software is installed in the machine. We will discuss these things in detail and practice as well.

The codes and software setup are important parts of learning. Without this, we will not be able to practice or implement our learning. Installation guide is the first equipment that an user requires to start the training for a new programming language.

Structure

In this chapter, we will discuss the following topics:

- Setting up our machine to run and write Java program
- JDK installation guide
- Setting the class path and environment variable
- Why class path is required
- Writing your first Java program

Objectives

After completion of this chapter, you will be able to:

- Install JDK and Java on your machine
- Set up class path and environment variable
- Execute the program written in Java

Installation

To install the JDK in our machine, we first need to download the JDK from the official Java website (**https://www.oracle.com/technetwork/java/javase/downloads/index.html**), based on the operating system and version which you want to install.

The following are the steps to install the JDK:

1. Go to the previously mentioned Oracle download center and download the latest version of compatible JDK for your machine. If you want a free version, then you can download Java 8 although higher versions are also free for students and practice purpose.

2. JDK is available to you in a single jar file. Unzip the downloaded ZIP file. Open the extracted folder and simply install Java by double-clicking on the **jdk-<version>.exe** file as showing in the following screenshot:

idealC-2021.1.1	01-05-2021 12:27	Application	6,59,025 KB
jdk-8u131-windows-x64	09-05-2017 07:51	Application	2,02,784 KB
MobaXterm_Portable_v21.0	14-04-2021 10:19	Compressed (zipp...	26,303 KB

***Figure 2.1**: Oracle JDK setup file*

a. Click **`Next`** and click the checkbox **`I agree for term and condition. And then finish installation`**:

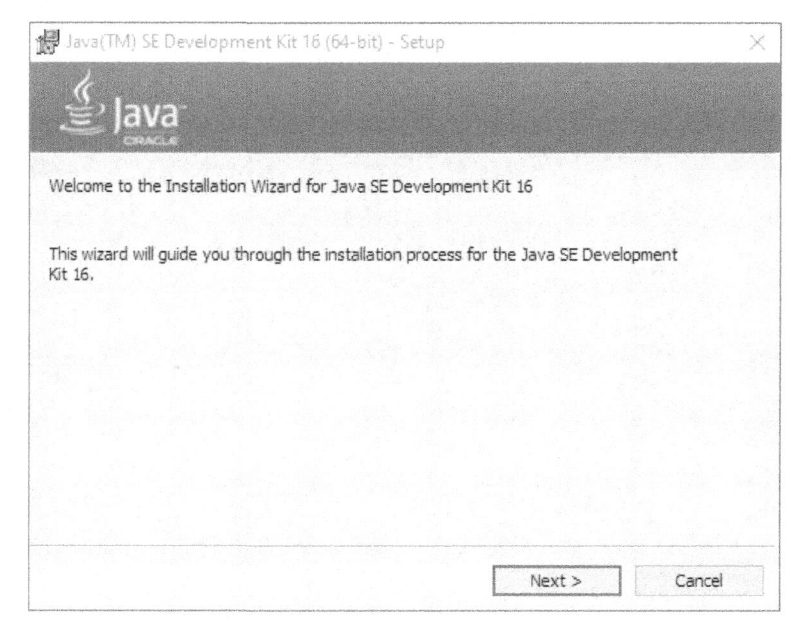

***Figure 2.2**: Java installation wizard*

b. "**`Java has been successfully installed`**" message will appear:

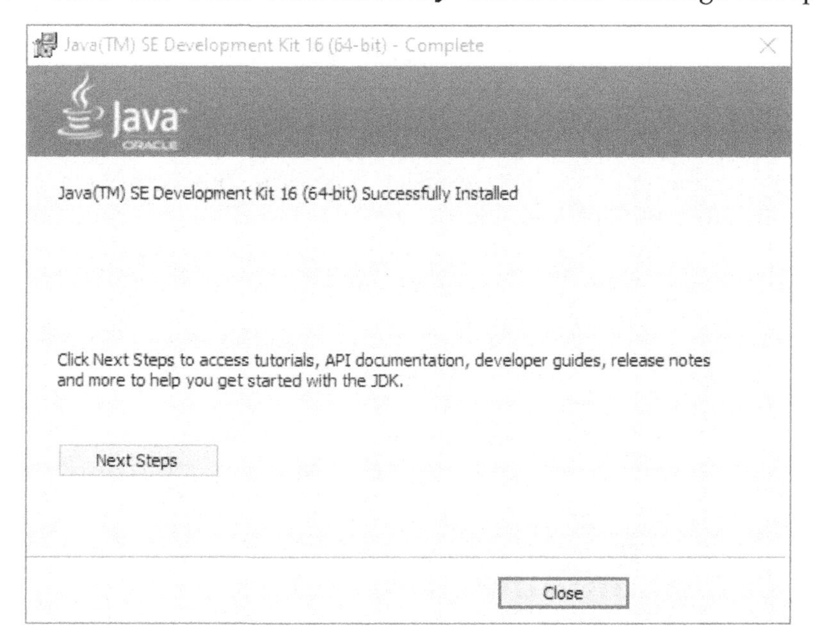

***Figure 2.3**: JDK successfully installed window*

After successful installation, check the installed version of Java in your machine using the command prompt (CMD). To do so, open CMD and type the command **`java -version`** as shown in the following *Figure 2.4*:

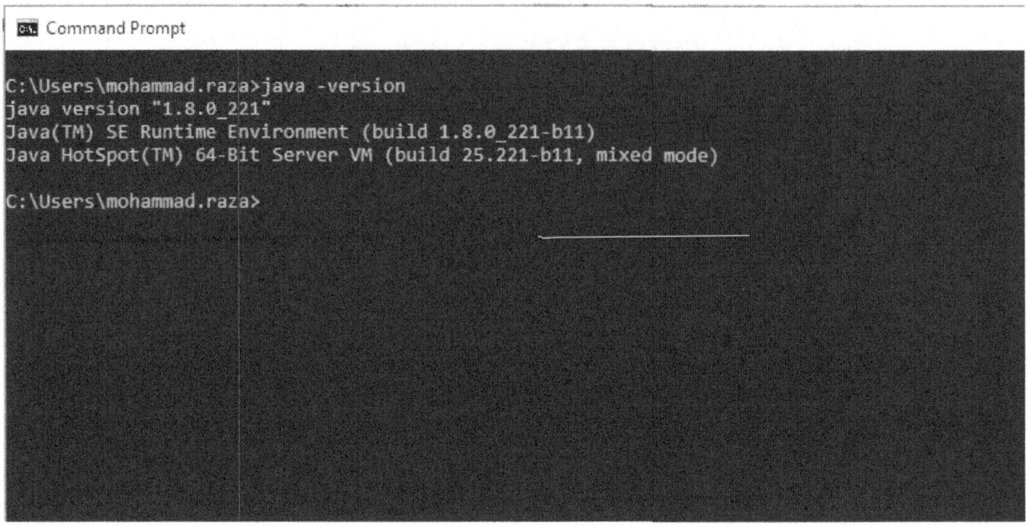

```
Command Prompt

C:\Users\mohammad.raza>java -version
java version "1.8.0_221"
Java(TM) SE Runtime Environment (build 1.8.0_221-b11)
Java HotSpot(TM) 64-Bit Server VM (build 25.221-b11, mixed mode)

C:\Users\mohammad.raza>
```

***Figure 2.4**: Check Installed Java Version in your machine*

The preceding snippet shows that this machine has Java installed and the version of Java is 1.8.0_221, along with JRE and JVM information.

Setting class path variable

When we write a program and try to compile using the Java compiler, the machine will look for JDK to compile and run the program. So, either we to have to specify the directory of the software library every time with our command or we could set it into an environment variable so that the machine can automatically pick up the library path from the environment variables based on the command. The environment variable holds the path of the software installed in our machine.

We set the variable JAVA_HOME to compile and run the Java programs:

```
JAVA_HOME = C:\Program Files\Java\jdk1.8.0_201
```

You may also directly set JDK path in the system **`CLASSPATH`** variable and **`PATH`** variable section under the environment variable. There are two ways to set the **`JAVA_HOME`** in a machine.

Using command line argument

Setting environment variable using the command line is easy and the fastest way to set. We can set using CMD in just two steps:

1. Open the command line (CMD). To open the CMD, click on the **`Start`** button and type CMD in search section of windows machine, then click on the command prompt to open the **command line interface** (**CLI**):

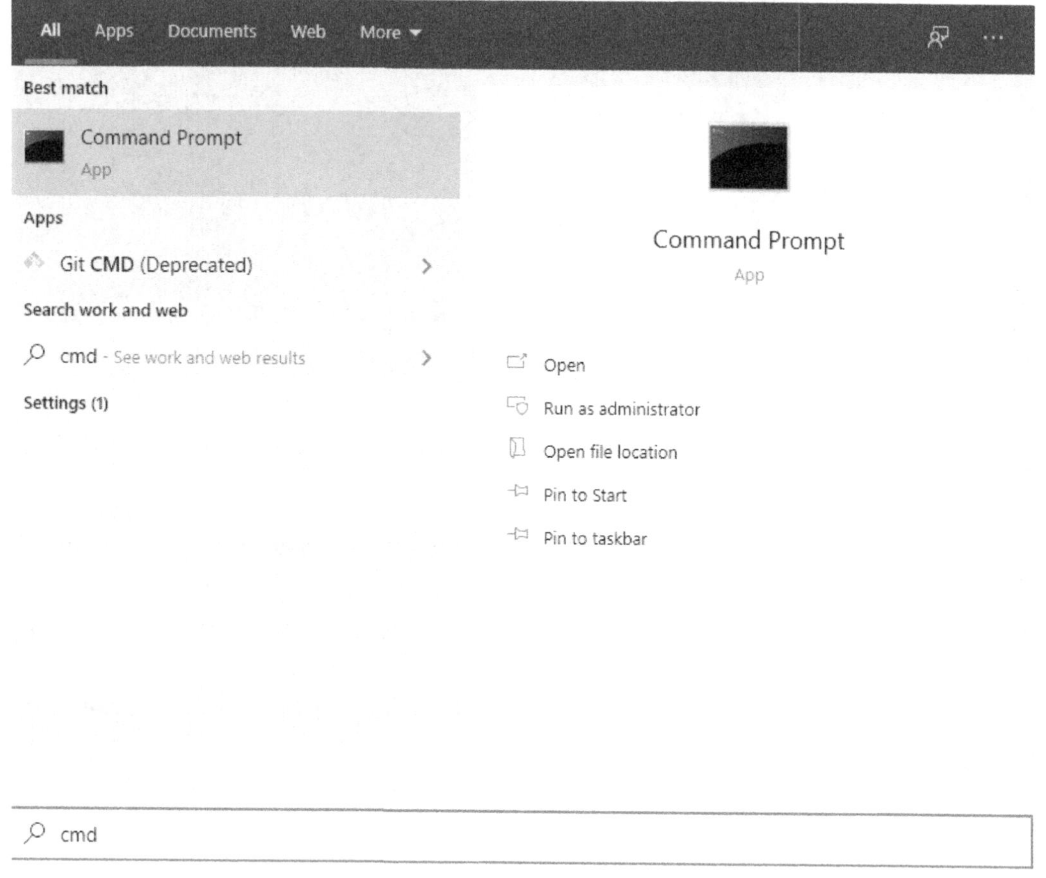

***Figure 2.5**: Open CMD in windows 10*

Another way to open the command prompt is go to **`Run`** and type **`cmd`** and then hit *Enter*, which will let you open the command line:

***Figure 2.6**: Open CMD using run option*

2. Hit the command:

   `setx -m JAVA_HOME post JDK path`

   For example: **`setx -m JAVA_HOME "C:\Progra~1\Java\jdk1.8.0_201"`**

```
Command Prompt
Microsoft Windows [Version 10.0.19042.1237]
(c) Microsoft Corporation. All rights reserved.

C:\Users\mohammad.raza>setx -m JAVA_HOME "C:\Progra~1\Java\jdk1.8.0_XX"
```

Figure 2.7: Set environment variable using command line

Using the GUI wizard

We can set the JAVA_HOME environment variable using wizard option also under **`MyComputer`** properties. The following are the steps to set an environment variable:

1. Right-click on **`My PC`** or **`My computer`** or **`This PC`**.
2. Go to the **`Properties`** option.
3. Click on **`Advanced system settings`** on the left-hand side as shown in *Figure 2.8*:

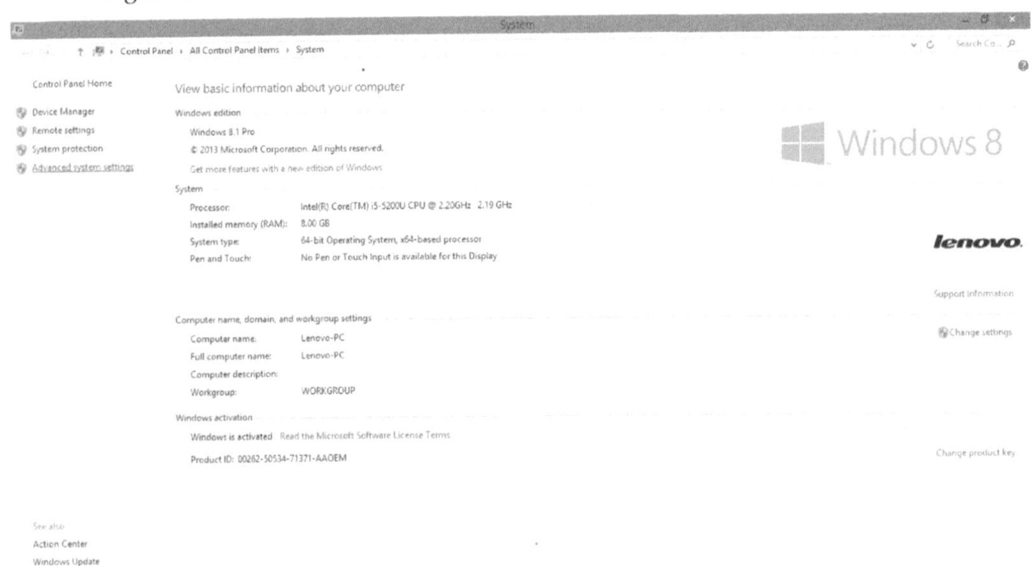

Figure 2.8: Windows settings

4. A new window will appear by the name **System Properties** as shown in the *Figure 2.9*. Now, click on the **Environment Variables** button at the bottom right of the window:

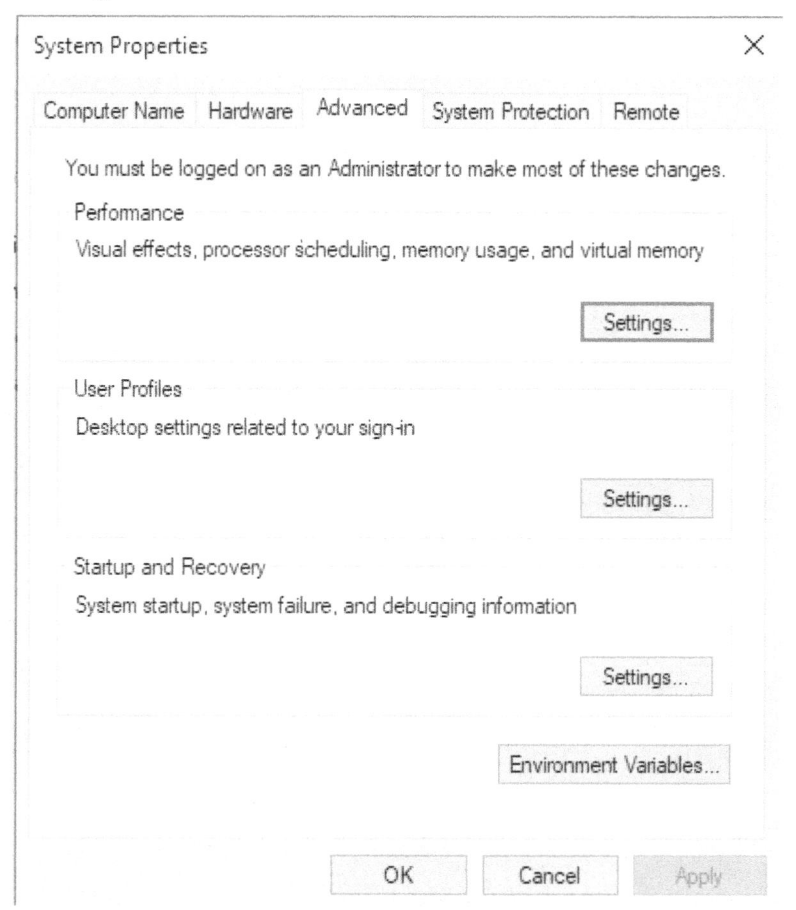

***Figure 2.9**: System properties window*

5. When you click on **Environment Variables**, a new window will pop up where you will see that all different kinds of variables are set.

6. You can set the **`Environment Variable`** directly under **`System Environment Variable`** or create a new variable under **`User Variables`** section and add the variable name in **`Path`** or **`CLASSPATH`** variable under **`System variables`** as shown in the *Figure 2.10*:

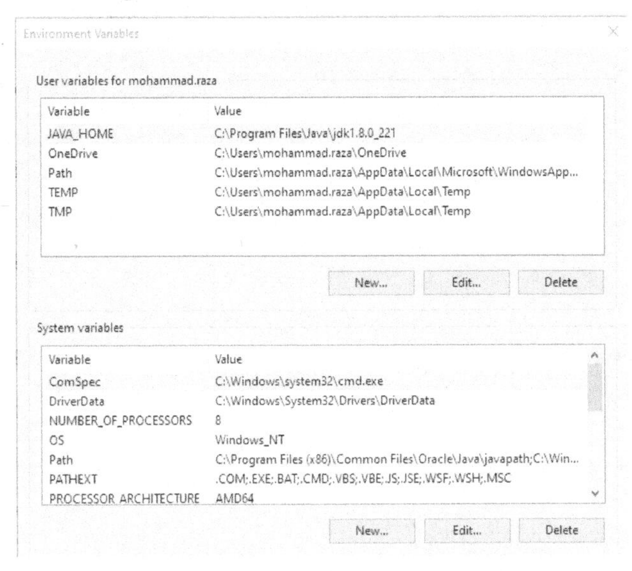

Figure 2.10: *Environment variables window*

7. To create a new variable, click on the **`New`** button and fill the variable name and variable value. You may also browse to the path of installed software as shown in the *Figure 2.11*:

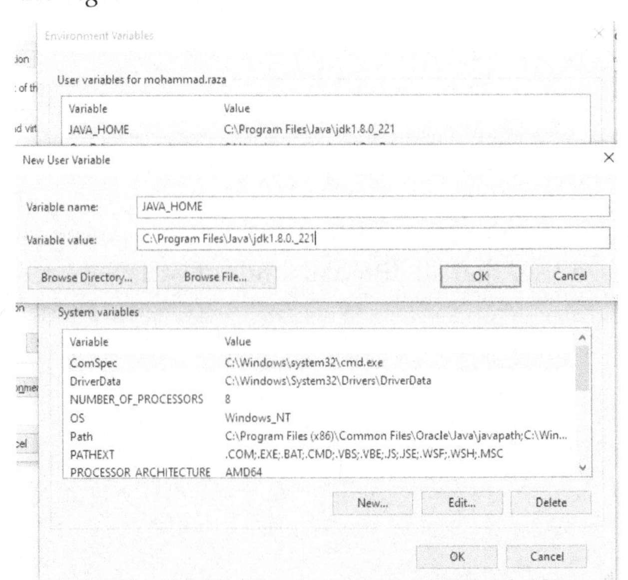

Figure 2.11: *New environment variable setup window*

8. To edit any existing variable or to include a newly created variable in the system variable path, simply select the variable and click on the **Edit** button to edit that variable. After this, you may update any existing value or add new variable and values into it as shown in the *Figure 2.12*:

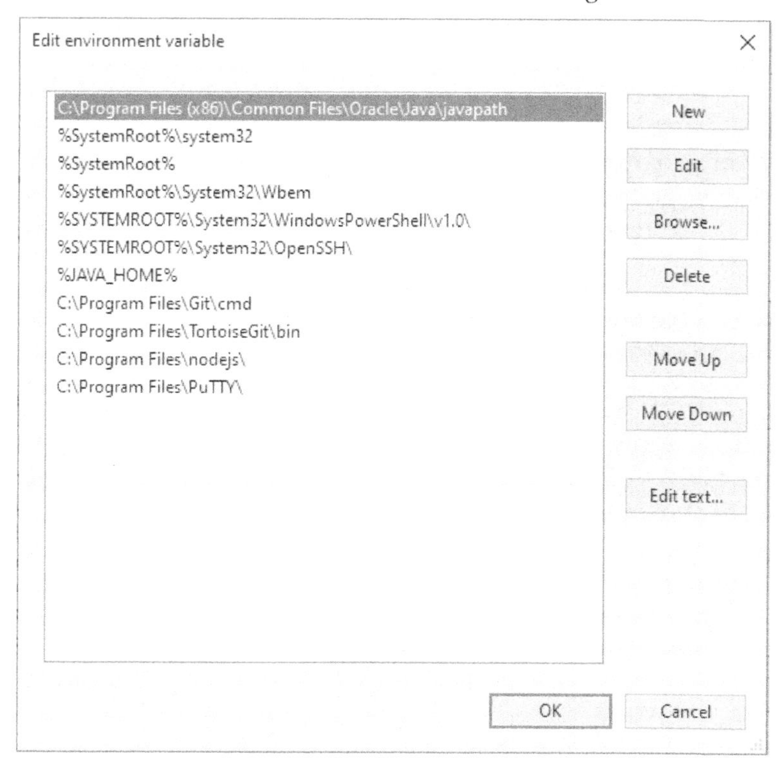

***Figure 2.12**: Edit environment variable*

9. After all changes, click on **OK** and then click on the **Apply** button.

We have successfully set the environment variable on the machine for Java class path. Now, our next action will be to write a simple Java program and get it executed.

Writing your first Java program

Let's start writing the first Java program to print the text "First Java program!":

1. Open the notepad and write the following code snippet. Save the file in a folder with the name **FirstJavaProgram.java**:

```
public class FirstJavaProgram {

  public static void main(String[] args) {
    System.out.println("First Java program!");
```

```
    }
}
```

2. Open the command prompt (CMD). To open the cmd, click on the **`Start/ Windows`** button and search for **`cmd`**. Then, click on the command prompt application.

   OR

   You can also open the cmd directly from Windows file explorer. Using **`File explorer`**, go to the folder where you have saved your Java program. On the address bar, type **`cmd`** and press *Enter*. It will pop up the command prompt for you.

3. Then run the Java compiler to compile your Java source code. To do so, type **`javac FirstJavaProgram.java`**.

4. Press *Enter*. It will compile your code into a bytecode and save into a .class file in the same directory. In our case, it will create **`FirstJavaProgram.class`** file. A **`.class`** file is unreadable for humans and the content of the file looks as shown in *Figure 2.13*:

```
FirstJavaProgram.class - Notepad
File  Edit  Format  View  Help
Êþº¾   4 "  FirstJavaProgram  java/lang/Object  <init>  ()V  Code
  LineNumberTable  LocalVariableTable  this  LFirstJavaProgram;  main  ([Ljava/lang/String;)V
java/lang/System  out  Ljava/io/PrintStream;  First Java program!
  java/io/PrintStream  println  (Ljava/lang/String;)V  args  [Ljava/lang/String;
SourceFile  FirstJavaProgram.java !          /     *· ±
                 7             ²   ±
                                  !
```

***Figure 2.13**: A snapshot of .class file*

5. After successfully compilation, to get the output of the program, run the command: **`java FirstJavaProgram`** as shown in the *Figure 2.14*:

***Figure 2.14**: Console output window*

By performing the preceding five steps, you have successfully executed a Java program in your machine. The last window as shown in *Figure 2.8* is the command prompt where you will get the output of your program.

Conclusion

In this chapter, we discussed and learnt how to prepare our machine for Java development. Java development kit (JDK) is a software development toolkit for Java, which we need to write and run the program and application written in Java programming language. In the previous chapter, we already discussed about the different parts of JDK and their roles, like JRE, JVM and JIT. You may refer those for revision and better understanding.

We also need to set up the environment variable or system variable, so that our machine has the reference of JDK and recognizes the Java commands and gets them executed on the Java class path.

In the next chapter, we will discuss the basics of programming and syntax of Java programming. When we start learning a language, we start with vocabulary. Similarly, Java also have so many words that we need to write a program. Those words are called keywords in programming language.

Points to remember

- JDK is a SDK and a prerequisite to work with Java, that needs to be installed in your machine.
- Source code compilation and interpretation is only handled by JDK.
- We need to set the environment variable so that the machine can automatically pick the library path to run the program or application.

Multiple choice questions

1. **Command javac is used to:**
    a. Debug the code
    b. Compile the Java source code
    c. Execute the Java program
    d. Write the Java program

2. **What is the file extension of a Java program file?**
    a. .java
    b. .javac
    c. .class
    d. .txt

Answers

1. **b**
2. **a**

Questions

1. What is the environment variable and why we need this?
2. How is .class file from .java file?

References

1. https://www.oracle.com/java/technologies/javase/jdk13-archive-downloads.html
2. https://www.oracle.com/technetwork/java/javase/downloads/index.html
3. https://www.java.com/en/download/help/path.xml
4. https://rashidjorvee.blogspot.com/2019/07/environment-variable.html

CHAPTER 3
Class, Object, and Variable

In this chapter, we will discuss the foundation and basics of the Java programming language. These are very important to study, write, and understand the source code in Java. Without knowledge of these terms and syntax, you will not be able to understand the concept and design of programming.

Structure

In this chapter, we will discuss the following topics:

- Classes
- Objects
    - Class loader
        - Bootstrap
        - Extension
        - System
- Packages
- Access modifiers/specifiers
    - Private
    - Public

- Protected
- Default

- Variables
  - Types of variables
    - Class variable
    - Instance variable
    - Local variable
    - Constant variable
- Data types
- Methods
- Methods with arguments
- Statements in Java
- Comments

Objectives

After completion of this chapter, you will be able to:

- Explain the class, design of a class, and the need to create class
- Explain the objects and their creation
- Understand the packaging or bundling of multiple source code files into a package
- Explain the class loader and what kind of class gets loaded into the memory and when and the significance of these class loaders
- Discuss the data type and its various types to store the different values and the default values for those data types
- Understand the access specifiers or modifiers that provide the scope and visibility to class, method, and variable
- Explain variables, different types of variables in Java programming, and their needs
- Understand the comments and ways available in Java to add comments in the source code
- Explain a statement and how to start and end a statement

A brilliant feature of object-oriented programming is to have a class. Classes play a vital role in keeping our code modular and scalable. We will discuss modular and scalable code in the upcoming chapters. In this chapter, we will learn how to create a class, the types of classes we can write, and how to use or reuse the class. Also, we will discuss the objects and create the object of a class using new keywords.

In programming, we need variables to store our data. For example, if we want to perform some operation, we store the result and provide values to operands through variables only. Here, we will also discuss how to create variables and what all data types are available to create a variable. Data types are the special meanings that tell a variable that this variable can store only a specific type of data with specific size. For example, an integer variable can only a store integer value and the char variable can store only the char value.

Using modifiers, it is possible to hide and expose the member of class. It provides the scope and visibility to a member. In this chapter, we will discuss the types of available modifiers like private, public, and protected and their roles.

Every line of code that we write is known as a statement and a statement always ends with a semicolon in Java programming.

In the comments, we will learn the significance of comments. The commented part of the code is never executed and compiled by the compiler. So, to give an understanding of any functionality to other programmer, we write some description with code. Also, we will comment those parts of the code which we do not want to execute.

Class

A class is a structure of object that is a combination of variables, methods, functional, and arithmetic operations. In class, we write all the operations using different operators and operands, and after successful execution, it will give the expected result.

Class can have different visibility, which sets the restriction and creates boundary for a class. Name of the class must start with a block letter as per the Java naming convention. Let's see how we create a Class in Java.

Syntax to declare class:

```
<access specifier/visibility> class <NameOfClass>{ }
```

For example:

```
public class JavaProgram {
  // Write your statement and operations here.
}
```

A class can also be declared with keywords such as abstract, interface and final. We use these keywords for different purposes and hold some unique features into it. These keywords are itself a topic. Hence, we will discuss in the upcoming chapters. Here, we will see how we might use these keywords to create a class.

A class can be empty or have a body. Body of a class is defined under the open and close curly braces. All statements, constructors, methods, and variables are only declared inside the body. Outside the body, we cannot declare anything.

```
public class ClassA {
// this is the body of a class, everything we will write inside this body only
}
```

A Java source code file may have more than one class. But there will be only one class which will be declared with a public modifier. Rest others could be private, abstract, and final.

Example 3.1: This all code is part of the single **`ExampleTest.java`** file:

```
package rashid.example.abc;
public class ExampleTest extends Base{

  public static void main(String[] args) {
    ExampleTestexampleTest = new ExampleTest();
    Base = new Base();
  }
}

class Base {
  private void MethodEx() {
    System.out.println("Base class method");
  }
}

abstract class NewMan {

}
```

Class members and methods are declared in the class using the **`static`** keyword. These members and methods are shared will all the instances of class. We could access a class member and method using the class name. There is no need to create an object of a class to access the class members. We will discuss more on this in the class variable section, later in this chapter.

Object

Objects are the real copy of a class, which we create in our program to work on or with the variable, method, constructor, and operation defined in the class. Every time we create an object, it creates a separate copy of that class and loads in the memory. Two objects can be identical in feature, but their memory management is completely different, and both will not mess with each other. Objects share the two characteristics - state and behavior. Every object has some state, and the state keeps changing. Also, objects have behavior and objects act differently on instructions. For example, a car is an object. The following could be the state and behavior of a car object:

State: halt, moving

Behavior: changing gear, starting, applying break, honking

We need the object to access and deal with the instance method and a member of the class. We cannot access an instance member of a class without creating an object of a class. The instance member is not loaded in the memory at the time of class load, but the memory of instance member will get allocated as soon we create the object/ instance of that class.

We create an object of a class using the **`new`** keyword. For example, we have a class **`NewYear`** and now we want to create two objects of this **`NewYear`** class:

```
NewYearobjectOne = new NewYear();
NewYearobjectTwo = new NewYear();
```

This is how we create an object of a class. Every time we need to write this statement with a new object name, create a new object of a class.

Class loader

Class loader is a part of JRE, which is responsible for loading every Java class file in the memory and make the bytecode available for JVM to execute on demand. The class **`ClassLoader`** is an abstract class. It gives the binary name of a class. In Java, libraries are available in an archive file format that is known as **Java Archive (JAR)**. The class loader is also responsible for loading the classes from internal and external library files. Each Java class must be loaded by a class loader to get executed.

Class loading is the most fascinating feature of Java programming. It focuses on loading, linking, and initializing the class and making the class available to be run by JVM. Loading of a class must be performed before linking and linking must be performed before initialization of a class in any Java program:

- **Loading**: Loading helps to locate the binary representation of a class and bring it into JVM.
- **Linking**: Linking is a process to take the class loaded by loading process and incorporate that type into runtime state/mode to get executed by JVM.
- **Initialization**: Initialization is the process to execute the object of that class.

Three class loaders were being used when Java virtual machines started. These are known as built-in class loaders.

Bootstrap class loader

The bootstrap class loader is responsible for loading the core Java library classes into Java virtual machine. Here, library is written in native Java and available in JRE under the **`/jre/lib`** directory. For example, java.*, javax.* , and so on. There is no parent for a bootstrap class loader, which is typically represented as null.

Extension class loader

- Extension class loader is responsible to load the classes from the library, which are present in JRE under the **`/jre/lib/ext`** extension directory, or any other directory specified by the **`java.ext.dirs`** system property. Any JAR file in the **`/jre/lib/ext`** directory is treated as an extension by **java runtime environment** (JRE).
- **`Java.ext.dirs`** is a general-purpose class loading mechanism that informs JRE where to load the extensions library classes.
- As of Java 6, extension JAR files may also be placed in a location that is independent of any JRE, so that the extensions can be shared by all JREs that are installed on a system. Prior to Java 6, the value of **`java.ext.dirs`** was referred to a single directory, but as of now, Java 6 is a list of directories (such as **CLASSPATH**) that specify the locations in which extensions are searched for. The first element of the path is always the **`lib/ext`** directory of the JRE. The second element is a directory outside the JRE. This other location allows extension JAR files to be installed once and used by several JREs installed on that system.

System class loader

System class loader is responsible to load the classes from system class path that is listed in the system environment variable **CLASSPATH**. You may refer to the set class path variable in the previous chapter for more detail. This is also known as application class loader.

Package

Package is a kind of bundle or container or library, where we put one or more Java classes, interfaces, and other related entities/information. It means bundling the multiple related program files at one place. Package is the first statement of any Java program.

To create the package, we just need to create a simple folder, and at the time of compilation, we should use the **-d** option and complete the directory name to compile the Java code:

```
javac -d C://java/com.example/program/SampleClass.java
```

Other ways to create a package using IDE such as eclipse/NetBeans is so easy. You can simply click on **file** >> **new** >> **package** and create your package.

The purpose of creating package is to organize the related entities at a single place. We can also set the visibility that means variable, fields, class, and method declared with default access specifier and can be accessible for all the classes within a package. Other modifier keywords such as private, public, protected work as they are designed. Package can also be utilized to separate two or more classes with the same name so that we can put one class in package A and another in package B as shown in *Figure 3.1*:

***Figure 3.1**: Package*

The preceding figure of package A and B are having an identical class car.java, but both the classes are treated as different.

We also provide a unique name of that package that is called namespace. Using this namespace, we use the functionality of classes and interfaces defined in that package. Syntax to put a class under a package:

```
package <name.of.package>
```

For example, **package org.bpb.program.sample;**

Package name should always be in lower case using dot (**.**) to separate the words.

In Java programming, importing keyword helps us to inject the package in our program and so we could make use of those classes.

For example:

```
import java.lang;
  import java.util.List; // to import just List class from package util.
  import java.util.*; // this will import all the classes from util
package. * represents all.
```

Java libraries come under the packages. For example, **java.util** and **java.lang** are the packages that provide different classes and interface using which we develop our programs. The following *Table 3.1* is for **java.lang** package, which includes the classes String, Math, List, Object, System, and many more:

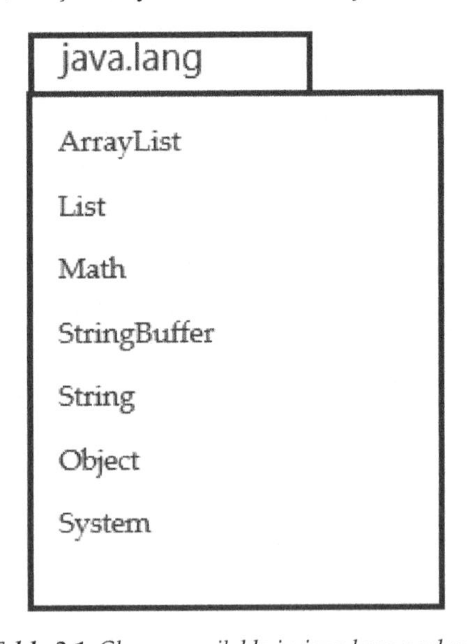

***Table 3.1**: Classes available in java.lang package*

Access specifier

Access specifier is a keyword that we use to set the visibility or scope or define the boundary of variable, method, and class. This is also known as modifier. There are four types of access specifiers in Java programming.

Private

Variable, method, and class declared private will be accessible only with the block { }. For example, if a private variable declares within a method, then that can only be accessible within the method body.

Example 3.2: Scope of a private variable:

```
public class ExampleTest {

  public void MethodEx() {
    private String firstName = "Priyank";
  }

  public static void main(String[] args) {
    ExampleTestexampleTest = new ExampleTest();
    exampleTest.firstName = "Raju"; // we cannot access this private
variable in main method.
  }
}
```

The preceding program will generate compilation error since we are trying to access a private member of the method **MethodEx**, **firstName** inside the main method.

Let's see another example to access declare and access the private method outside the class:

Example 3.3: Scope of the private method:

```
package rashid.example.abc;
public class ExampleTest extends Base{

  public static void main(String[] args) {
    ExampleTestexampleTest = new ExampleTest();
    Base base = new Base();
    base.MethodEx();
  }
}

class Base {
  private void MethodEx() {
    System.out.println("Base class method");
  }
}
```

The preceding program will generate compilation error on line **base.MethodEx();**. "The method **MethodEx()** from the type Base is not visible" because we are trying to access a private member of base class, which can only be accessed within the Base class not by any other class, including the class which inherits the base class.

Public

Public modifier makes everything public. The variable, method, and class declared with public modifier can be accessible to any class and method. There is no restriction and boundary defined for public.

Protected

Access modifier **Protected** is in between private and public. It allows the access to all classes within the same package and classes that are subclasses of other classes. Here, derived or subclass means protected will allow to inherit the properties from base class or parent class.

Let us design two classes **ParentClass** and **ChildClass**. **ChildClass** inherits the **ParentClass**. So, all the properties other than private can be accessible by **ChildClass**. Following is the program:

```
Class ParentClass
package rashid.example.abc;
public class ParentClass {
  protected String cityName = "New Delhi";
  protected String surname = "Raza";

}
Class ChildClass
package rashid.example.abc;
public class ChildClass extends ParentClass {

  public static void main(String[] args) {
    ChildClasschildClass = new ChildClass();
    System.out.println(childClass.cityName);
    System.out.println(childClass.surname);
  }
}
```

In the preceding example, **ParentClass** has two protected variables **cityName** and **surname**. A normal class might not be able to access the protected members of other classes. However, by using inheritance, when we inherit a class using the extends keyword, that inherited class exposes all its variables and methods to the derived class. This creates a relationship between two classes, as in real world we have relation with our father. And we do have rights to access the assets belonging to our father. We will discuss more about base and derived class in the Inheritance chapter.

Default

Default is the default access modifier when we do not write any modifier with class declaration. Default modifier makes a class accessible within the same package.

Variable

Variable is a unique name that represents and holds a value. Variable could be any valid name (based on the certain naming convention) or it could be your name also. A Java keyword can't be a variable; for example, public, abstract, interface; we cannot create a variable with these names. For a complete list of Java keywords, please refer to the Java keyword section at the end of this chapter.

Name of a person is like a variable that represents a human. When someone calls a name, then instantly as a value an image has been created in our mind, which represents Mr X.

Java has certain naming conventions for a valid variable. These naming conventions help other developers to understand the code written by a developer. A Java variable should always start with or the first character should always be an English alphabet (A to Z or a-z), number (0 to 9), dollar sign ($), and underscore (_). We cannot start a variable name other than these three types of chars.

The syntax to declare a variable are as follows:

```
<access specifier><data type><variableName>
```

For example:

```
  private String firstName = "Rajan";
    private int marks = 350;
```

In March 2018, Java released its new version Java 10. Java 10 onwards, we have one more easy way to declare the variable using the var keyword. The benefit of the **var** keyword is that we need not specify the data type while declaring the variable. Based on the assigned value, the system will automatically assign the required data type to hold that value. For example:

```
var firstName = "Mohit";
```

The value of this variable is string type; hence, the variable firstName automatically assigns it the data type String.

```
var age = 8; // this variable age will created consider as a type of
integer
```

One disadvantage of the var declaration is that it does not allow compound declaration. We cannot declare more than one variable in a single statement separated by comma (,).

Invalid declaration:

```
var firstName  = "Mohammad", lastName = "Raza";
```

To declare multiple variables, we need to right each variable in a new statement.

For example:

```
var firstName  = "Mohammad";
var lastName = "Raza";
```

A sample program to divide two numbers using **var** declaration:

```
public class VarExample {
    public static void main(String args[]) {
       var a = 5;
       var b = 6;
       var c = b/a;
       System.out.println(c);
    }
}
```

Types of variables

There are different types of variables, which can be used for different purposes. Let's understand the types of variables in detail.

Class variable

Class variables are those variables, which are declared at the class level and all the instances of that class are going to share the same variable with the same value. If any instance updates the value of a class variable, the same will be updated for all the instances of that class. It is not a good practice to update the value of any class variable by any program. The variables that have a fixed value should be declared as class variables. We declare the class variable using a static keyword. The static keyword ensures that only one instance of this variable will be created. The class variable is also known as static variable. Below is an example of variable declaration and assignation.

```
static int age = 5;
```

If you don't assign any value in a static variable and further use that variable to perform some operation in your program, then it will give you the default value of that variable based on specified default values for that data type.

Example 3.4: Default value assignation by JVM

For example:

```
public class StaticVariable {
  static int age;
  public static void main(String[] args) {
    System.out.println(age);

  }
}
```

The preceding program will run successfully and print 0, which is the default value for `int` in Java.

NOTE: Anything declared using static keyword gets loaded in the memory at the time the class gets loaded. Static is not dependent on object initialization. Hence, class variable is always declared as a static.

Constant variable

Constant variables are those variables that are fixed and once you assign a value to it, you cannot change it. It will remain the same always. If you try to reassign or update the value of the final variable, the compiler will generate an error message for you "**`The final field FinalVariable.XYZ cannot be assigned`**". Keywords that make a variable constant are final. It is recommended that you write a constant variable name in capital letters and use only underscore to separate the two words.

For example:

```
   <access specifier> final <data type><VARIABLE_NAME>
public final String USER_NAME = "Value";
```

Example 3.5: A sample program to create a constant variable:

```
public class FinalVariable {
  final int AGE = 5;

  public void AccessVariable() {
    System.out.println(AGE);
  }
  public static void main(String[] args) {
    FinalVariablefinalVariable = new FinalVariable();
    finalVariable.AccessVariable();
  }
}
```

NOTE: If a primitive type or string is defined as a constant, the program will replace that constant with an assigned value everywhere in the code at the time of compilation. We may also refer to constant as a compile-time constant.

Instance variable

Instance variables are declared outside the methods, constructors, and any code blocks. There is separate memory allocation for each instance, and every instance will deal with its own copy of instance variable. Instance variables can only be accessible by creating the object of a class. This is also called non-static variable.

Instance variable is declared at the same place where we declare class variable, but here, we do not use static keyword to declare the variable:

```
public class InstanceVariable {
  int zip=110019;
  public static void main(String[] args) {
    System.out.println(zip);


  }
}
```

We cannot use the instance variable on non-static field without creating the object of the class. To access a non-static variable and field, we must update our program by creating the instance of the class and call the variable using the object as follows:

Example 3.6: Instance variable:

```
public class InstanceVariable {
  int zip;
  public static void main(String[] args) {
    InstanceVariable instanceVariable = new InstanceVariable();
    System.out.println(instanceVariable.zip);


  }
}
```

Now, let's create the two objects of the **`InstanceVariable`** class and update the value for variable zip and fetch the value using the object of class:

```
public class InstanceVariable {
  int zip;


  public static void main(String[] args) {
```

```
    InstanceVariable instanceVariable = new InstanceVariable();
    instanceVariable.zip=11002;
    InstanceVariable instanceVariableTwo = new InstanceVariable();
    instanceVariableTwo.zip=44001;

    //Now access the variable zip using the different instances.
    System.out.println(instanceVariable.zip);
    System.out.println(instanceVariableTwo.zip);
  }
}
```

Output:

```
11002
44001
```

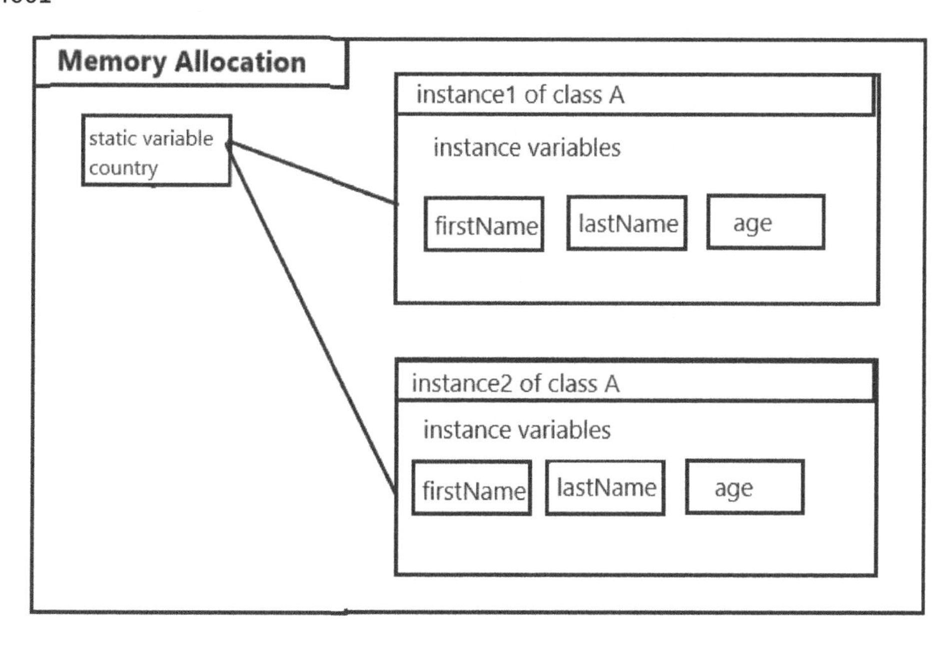

Figure 3.2: Memory allocation of static and non-static variables

Local variable

Local variables are private variables or variables declared with private visibility or variables received as an argument of a method. The scope is quite limited for these variables and are removed from memory after execution of that method or block. It is compulsory to assign the local variable. If you use the variable that is not assigned any value, then you will get a compile time error "`The local variable xyz may`

`not have been initialized`". Local variables do not get assigned with default value of data type as class and instance variables.

Example 3.7: Local variable:

```
public class LocalVariable {

  public static void main(String[] args) {
    String lastName;
    System.out.println(lastName);

  }
}
```

When you try to compile the preceding program, it will not compile and generate compilation error.

To fix the compilation error in the program, assign some value to the variable **`lastName`**.

Set explicitly

We can also set the visibility and scope of a variable using access specifiers - public, private, and protected. You may refer Access specifier section to understand more about these keywords and their boundaries.

Parameter

Variable which a method receives as an argument is called a parameter variable; the scope of this variable remains till the closing of the same method body. Let's understand this with an example.

Example 3.8: Argument or parameter variable:

```
public class ParameterVariable {
  void MethodOne(String userName) { // this method received variable
userName
    System.out.println(userName);
  } // After this method closing braces, username will not accessible.
  public static void main(String[] args) {
    ParameterVariable pv = new ParameterVariable();
    pv.MethodOne("Mr. X");


  }
}
```

Data type

Data types are special representations of variables; it helps the compiler identify the value stored by the variable, and what all operation can be possible on that. For different types of copy, we have different data types to handle it. Once we declare a variable with a data type, then after that only we can store that type of value into that variable. Based on the data type, the system also allocates space in the memory. We cannot assign a String value into a number data type.

In Java programming, we have two types of data types.

Primitive data types

A primitive data type is a predefined data type that has a definite range of value to hold and what could be the default value if the user does not assign any value into it. The name of these data types are reserved with keyword. There are eight primitive data types supported by Java programming language. They are as follows:

1. **`byte`**: The **`byte`** data type is a 8-bit signed two's complement integer. Don't get confuse here with two's complement; two's complement is fixed point binary values. A variable declared byte can hold a minimum of 128 and a maximum 127 value. The byte data type is used to store small integers and is useful for memory saving.

   `short`: The short data type is 16-bit signed two's complement integer. It has a minimum value of -32,768 and a maximum value of 32,767. All other guidelines are same as byte.

2. **`int`**: The int data type is 32-bit signed two's complement integer. It has a minimum value of –2147483648 and a maximum value of 2147483647. In Java SE 8 and later, you can use the int data type to represent an unsigned 32-bit integer, which has a minimum value of 0 and a maximum value of 2^{32}-1. Use the Integer class to use int data type as an unsigned integer.

3. **`long`**: The long data type is 64-bit 2's complement integer. We use long data type when we need to store larger value, which is not possible to store in int. The signed long has a minimum value of -2^{63} and a maximum value of 2^{63}-1. In Java SE 8 and later, you can use the long data type to represent an unsigned 64-bit long, which has a minimum value of 0 and a maximum value of 2^{64}-1. To write a long value, it is recommended to write l (small letter of L) or L at the end of value; for example, *long telephone = 009191919191911L;*

4. **`float`**: The float data type is a single-precision 32-bit IEEE 754 floating point, where we could store the exact and accurate number with decimal. We use in the place of byte and short to handle the precise value. float can represent a decimal value up to 6 to 7 digits of precision. This data type should never

be used for precise values, such as currency. For that, you will need to use the **java.math.BigDecimal** class instead. Numbers and Strings cover BigDecimal and other useful classes provided by the Java platform. To write a float value, it is recommended that you write f or F at the end of value; for example, **floatpercentage = 23.674f;**

5. **double**: The double data type is a double-precision 64-bit IEEE 754 floating point. This is the first choice to store decimal number. We should use double in place of int and long to handle the decimal numbers. Double can represent decimal value up to 16 digits of precision. To write a double value, it is recommended to write d or D at the end of value; for example, **double pec=52731632.32462438891d;**

6. **char**: The char data type is a single 16-bit unicode character. It has a minimum value of **'\u0000'** (or 0) and a maximum value of **'\uffff'** (or 65,535 inclusive). We write the char value in between the single quotes ''. For example, **char firstAlpha = 'A';**

7. **boolean**: The Boolean data type is 1-bit data type, which has only two possible values, true and false. We use this data type to set a flag and check the condition. For example, **boolean flag = true;**

8. **String**: In addition to these eight primitive data types, Java provides one more data type String to support the character string. This String data type can be used in Java program by importing the **java.lang.String** class. Strings are constant; their values cannot be changed after they are created. We write the String value within the double quotes "". Enclosing your character string within double quotes will automatically create a new String object; for example, **String s = "You are learning Java.";** and **String s = new String("You are learning Java");**

Default value of primitive data types

Data Type	Default Value (for fields)	Bit signed	Minimum and maximum value
boolean	False	1 bit	true or false
byte	0	8 bit	-128 to 127
short	0	16 bit	-32,768 to 32,767
int	0	32 bit	-231 to 231-1
long	0L	64 bit	-263 to 263-1

float	0.0f	32 bit	1.4E-45 to 3.4028235E38
double	0.0d	64 bit	4.9E-324 to 1.7976931348623157E308
char	'\u0000'	16 bit	'\u0000' to '\uffff'
String	Null		

Table 3.2: data types and their detail information

Reference data type

Reference data type holds the reference of an object and this can be used with class, interface, array, and enum. The reference type doesn't hold any actual value; it always refers to and is dependent on other objects to get and set the values.

Literal

Literals are used to declare constant variables; you may notice we don't need to create an object using a new keyword to assign value to primitive type variables. For example, **`String name = "Mohan Das";`** is a string type literal.

A literal is the source code representation of a fixed value; literals are represented directly in your code without requiring computation.

- **Boolean literal:** Boolean literal has only two possible values; **`true`** and **`false`**. For example:

  ```
  boolean status = true;
  ```

- **Integer literal:** We may put an integer value in literal in different formats. Integer literals permit int and long type of data type. For example:

  ```
  int score = 320;
  long population = 12321322L;
  ```

- **Floating literal:** Floating literals are the constant variables that hold the decimal and exponential values and we may declare using float and double data types. For example:

  ```
  float number = 12.321F;
  double number = 21313.234223D;
  ```

- **Underscore char in number literal:** We use underscore character to separate the long numeric digits (as we put comma (,) or space ( ) between the numbers group), for better understanding and readability. Underscore between the numeric values will get ignored by the compiler.

```
long mobileNumber = 99999_99999L;
float salary = 12_523.98f;
```

- Character literal: Char literal is defining the single char value within the single quotes.

```
char attendance = ‘P’;
```

- String literals: Apart from primitive data types, there is one more literal of type String.

```
String name = “Rashid”;
```

- null: There is also a special literal null; null could be assigned as a value to any reference type to check the availability for that reference.

NOTE: The Java programming language also supports a few special escape sequences for char and String literals: \b (backspace), \t (tab), \n (line feed), \f (form feed), \r (carriage return), \" (double quote), \' (single quote), and \\ (backslash).

Method

The concept of method in programming language is not new; we have been writing methods in almost all programming languages. In simple real-world example, a method denotes a set of operations, and can have n number of tasks or may have many steps and instructions. So, combining multiple things together or bundling set of instructions for a single task and giving it a unique identification name is called method. For example, admission is a method. When we say admission, it means we will enroll in some program. However, admission is not only one thing, it is the complete process to get yourself enrolled for a program. Let us understand it in more simple terms.

In the admission process, we have to follow these steps:

1. Visit the center or portal.
2. Fill up the registration form.
3. Select your program.
4. Appear for the test/exam, if applicable.
5. Pay the admission fees.
6. Get the acknowledgment receipt.

The preceding six steps are a part of admission; so, when we say admission, it means we must complete these six steps for the process to be completed.

Similarly, in programming we declare methods; a method name should clearly represent what this is going to do, and what is the purpose of this method, and what we will achieve after this method. Within the method body, we write the related statements and operations that we want to perform. In our case, all the five steps of admission will be written under the body of method admission. So, whenever any user calls for admission, all five steps get executed and the user gets successfully enrolled for a program.

The method name could be any name, but it should be a name of java keyword. Refer to Java keywords section later in this chapter.

Syntax of method declaration:

```
<access specifier><return type><methodName>() {
}
```

For example:

```
private void admission() {
  visit center;
  fill registration form;
  ….
  …
}
```

Return type is mandatory for a method; this return type denotes what output or result we will receive after successful execution of this method. We use data types as a return type of the method. If your method is not going to return any data or result, then it must be declared with return type void which means null.

Parentheses `()` after the method name is compulsory.

Method body starts with opening curly braces **{** and ends with ending curly braces **}**, as the class body does. Statements written outside the body will not be treated as a part of the method.

Calling a method is simple. We just need to write the name of the method within parentheses `()`, if we are calling method in the same class. Or if you declare your method static, then you can call your method with the help of class name. Or if you are accessing an instance method, then call the method with the help of object or instance name. Refer to the following *Figure 3.3*.

For example:

- **Method within the same class:** **`methodName();`**

- **Instance method**: **`classObject.methodname();`**
- **Static method**: **`ClassName.methodName();`**

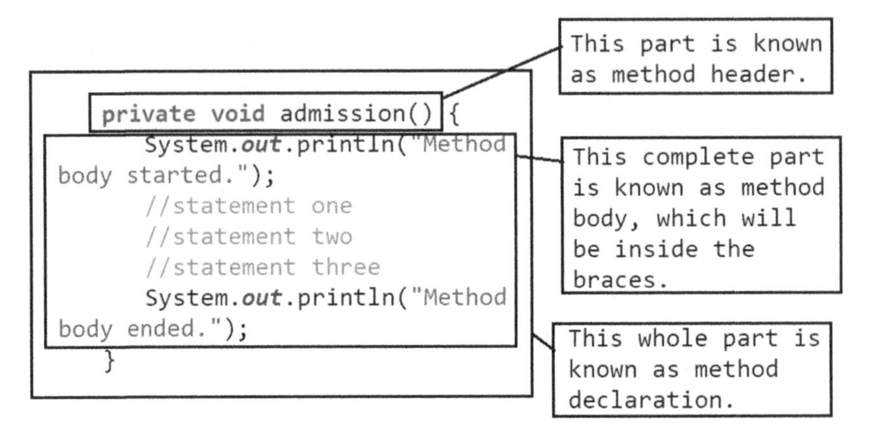

Figure 3.3: Calling a method

Example 3.9: Method with and without return statement:

```
public class MethodExample {
  private String withReturnType() {
    System.out.println("Method with return type.");
    return "Rashid";
  }
  private void withoutReturnType() {
    System.out.println("Method without return type.");
  }
  public static void main(String[] args) {
    MethodExample example = new MethodExample();
    String UserName = example.withReturnType();
    System.out.println(UserName);
    example.withoutReturnType();


  }
}
```

Output:

```
Method with return type.
Rashid
```

```
Method without return type.
```

Method with arguments

A method can have arguments as well; we can pass any number of arguments or parameters in a method. Here is a sample example of method with arguments. In the upcoming method overloading and overriding chapter, we will discuss more about this in depth.

Example 3.10: Method with an argument:

```
public class MethodExample {
  private String withReturnType(String name) {
    System.out.println("Method with return type name = " +name);
    return name;
  }
  private void withoutReturnType(int number) {
    System.out.println("Method without return type value: " +number);
  }
  public static void main(String[] args) {
    MethodExample example = new MethodExample();
    String UserName = example.withReturnType("Alice");
    System.out.println(UserName);
    example.withoutReturnType(5);

  }
}
```

Output:

```
Method with return type name = Alice
Alice
Method without return type value 5
```

Statement

A line of code or multiple lines of code that needs to be executed in one go is known as statement in programming. A statement ends and terminates with a semicolon (;). We can write more than one statement in a single line and one statement in multiple line.

```
int score = 5; String firstName=  "John"; Class obj = new Class(); obj.
Execute();
```

Here in the preceding line, we have written four statements, first is declaring the int literal variable score with value 5. Second is string literal with value John. Third is creating object or instance of Class. And fourth is calling an instance method **`Execute()`**. All these will get executed one by one since these four are distinct statements.

```
Class Mainclassmain =
new ClassMain(System.in);
```

The preceding two lines of code are just one statement and gets executed in one go. JVM will look for the termination point of statement, adds everything that comes before the semicolon (;) and is considered as one statement and executes it in one go.

Comment

Comments are a very good feature and they do not get compiled and executed. Interpreter or compiler ignore the things that are under the comments section. We use the comments for many meaningful purposes in Java source code. It makes our code readable and understandable for other developers who will work later the same code written by us. For a scalable system design, it is very important to put the comments. Comments can be used to:

- Add the method and class definition where we let a programmer know what this class and method is going to do and, what this will return and what all arguments are required to call this method
- Add the name of author in your source code
- Explain the constant variable
- Line of code or block of code which we do not want to execute

There are three ways to put comments in java source code. One is single liner comment, and another is multiline comment and third is Javadoc comment:

- **Single line comment:** Single line comment is to write a short comment. A single line comment can be written followed by double forward slash:

  // comment

- **Multiline comment:** Multiline comment is to write a short notes or explanation of the code. Multiline comment can be written starting with a forward slash and asterisk symbol and closing with forward slash followed by asterisk symbol. There are two ways to write multiline comments in Java source code; following are the syntax:

```
/*
comments
*/
```

OR

```
/*
*Comments
*comments
*/
```

- **Javadoc comment:** The Javadoc comment is a special comment generated by Javadoc tool for class, interface, and method. It contains definition and explanation of some common elements used in the interface and method. This is generally done when we create any API or public facing class and method. The JDK Javadoc tool uses doc comments when preparing automatically generated documentation.

  Elements that Javadoc include in this comment are:

  - **`@return`**: This indicates what this class and method will return you back.
  - **`@param`**: This indicates how many parameters a program must pass to use this method or class and what are the types of those.
  - @throw: throw indicates what error and exception this class and method is going to throw, so you could handle that at your end.
  - @since: since works only with core API class and method, which indicates this class and method is available in Java since version xx.

```
/**
*
*
*/
e.g.   /**
   * @param name
   * @return String
   */
  private String withReturnType(String name) {
    return name;
  }
```

Java keywords

Java keywords are meaningful predefined built-in keywords in language. Each keyword has its own feature and terms to use. We cannot use just these keywords as identifiers to name a variable, method, and class. Following are the Java keywords:

- `abstract`
- `break`
- `case`
- `catch`
- `class`
- `continue`
- `do`
- `double`
- `else`
- `enum`
- `exception`
- `extends`
- `final`
- `float`
- `for`
- `implements`
- `instanceof`
- `int`
- `interface`
- `long`
- `main`
- `new`
- `out`
- `private`
- `protected`
- `public`
- `return`

- `static`
- `String`
- `super`
- `switch`
- `system`
- `this`
- `throws`
- `try`
- `var`
- `void`
- `while`

Conclusion

Class is a blueprint or template to put the variable, method, constructor together in a structured way. Classes can also be used to separate the code file and divide the long file into smaller files. We need objects to access the instance/non-static variable or method of a class. A class can have any number of objects. Data type is the special reference that helps the compiler identify the possible value and operation on that identifier (also known as variable). Java packages are the bundles where we put multiple files (based on functionality and relation) and give a unique package name so that we can refer it as a one. The different types of variables are constant variables, instance variables, local variables, argument variables, static variables, and class variables.

Class loader is a part of JRE that is responsible to load each Java class file in memory and make the bytecode available for JVM to execute on demand. Three types of class loaders are bootstrap, executive and system. There are some Java keywords that have special meaning in Java programming; we cannot use these keywords as an identifier. It is illegal to use those identifiers to any variable, method, and class. In the next chapter, we will discuss constructors. Constructors are methods with no return type, and constructors are members of class and get executed when object of a class get created.

Points to remember

- Java is a case sensitive language; name should be treated identical only when it is written in the same case. The **`firstName`** and **`firstname`** are two different variable names in Java.

- We cannot use Java keywords as identifier names.
- There are four types of modifiers that can be used to set the visibility.
- We cannot access instance member of a class without creating object of that class.

Multiple choice questions

1. **Which is valid variable name?**
   a. +yourName
   b. xXyt
   c. #67te
   d. @firstname

2. **Which is a valid syntax to declare a class?**
   a. Class ClassName
   b. class SampleProgram
   c. AddTwoNumber class
   d. Public Class ExampleP

3. **Which is not a valid variable name?**
   a. $youname
   b. 9812For
   c. &age
   d. _00Name

4. **Can we create two objects of same class?**
   a. Yes
   b. No

5. **Which is the correct statement to create an object of class JavaProgram?**
   a. JavaProgramjp;
   b. JavaProgramjp = new JavaProgram;
   c. JavaProgram 0Pr = new JavaProgram();
   d. JavaProgramjavaPro = new JavaProgram() { };

6. **Which is the not a valid way to write comment in java source code?**
   a. //* this is a constant variable
   b. /* write your comment here */
   c. /* write your text
      *
      * this method will return zero;
      */
   d. **/

Answers

1. b
2. b
3. c
4. a
5. c
6. d

Questions

1. What all types of access modifiers are available in Java?
2. What is the difference between public and protected modifiers?
3. How instance variable is different from class variable?
4. Why can't we use java keywords for an identifier?
5. What is object and how to create an object of a class?
6. What are the 32-bit data types?
7. What are methods? What is a method header?
8. What is statement in Java programming?

Key terms

- **Identifier**: A name that uniquely identifies a variable, class, and method.
- **Modifier**: Access modifier or access specifier to set the visibility of an identifier.

- **Derived class**: A class that inherits the property of other classes.

Exercise

Exercise 1: Create a class with static members and access those members with class name to print the value.

1. Create a class with name MobileDevice.
2. Add the following static members in the class:
   A. A String variable deviceName to store the name of device
   B. A String variable manufacturedBy to store the company name
   C. A int variable price to store the price of device
   D. A method with name feature, which will print the description of that device.
3. Under the main method of class MobileDevice print the value of variables and description from method.

References

- https://docs.oracle.com/javase/tutorial/java/nutsandbolts/datatypes.html
- https://docs.oracle.com/javase/tutorial/java/data/numberformat.html
- https://docs.oracle.com/javase/tutorial/ext/basics/install.html
- https://docs.oracle.com/javase/9/docs/api/java/lang/ClassLoader.html
- https://www.oracle.com/technetwork/java/javase/documentation/codeconventions-141999.html

CHAPTER 4
Constructor

Constructor is a special type of method with the same name as the class name. Constructor is used in various ways to declare the default variable and load or make available the prerequisites of a program so that our program can execute smoothly. In this chapter, we will learn about the constructor and its role in programming.

Structure

In this chapter, we will discuss the following topics:

- Constructor
- Parameterized constructor
- Default constructor
- Super
- This

Objectives

After successful completion of this chapter, you will be able to:

- Explain the constructor and its different types
- Understand the use of super and the keywords

Constructor

A constructor is a special type of method in programming, which we use to initialize the member variables and member objects. Name of the constructor and class should always be the same, constructor postfixes with a parenthesis "()". The constructor does not have a return type. When we write return type with constructor, that will no longer remain a constructor and the compiler will consider it as a method with a warning message. The following is the statement to write a constructor:

```
Public class ConstructorExample {
  ConstructorExample() {
    // A constructor with name ConstructorExample
}
}
```

The purpose of creating constructor in a program is to initialize the member variables and member functions. Initialization means assigning some value to it. We also use a constructor to create the object of dependent classes and interfaces or prerequisites, which we need further in our program to complete the operation. The constructor gets called automatically or implicitly as soon as we create an object of a class. There can be more than one constructor in a class, there is no limit. We can overload the constructor based on the constructor signature, that is, the type of parameter, number of parameters, and sequence of parameters passed as argument in constructor. We will discuss more on this topic in the parameterized construction section later in this chapter.

We can restrict the visibility of the constructor by adding private access specifier so that it can only be accessed within the same class. The other classes will be unable to reach or call a private constructor. By default, the constructor is public:

```
ConstructorName() { // this is a public constructor
}

private ConstructorName() { // this is a private constructor
}
```

A constructor can't be static, final, and abstract. We can only declare private, protected, and public constructor.

Constructor can be either default or parameterized. Let us discuss more on the type of constructors.

Default constructor

A constructor with no parameter is treated as the default constructor. Every time we create an object of a class using the **new** keyword, we initialize the default constructor. After this, the system implicitly calls the constructor with no parameter written in the program:

```
Line 1: public class DefaultConstructor {
Line 2:
Line 3:   DefaultConstructor() {
Line 4:     //write your statement here
Line 5:   }
Line 6:
Line 7:   public static void main(String[] args) {
Line 8:     DefaultConstructor = new DefaultConstructor();
Line 9:
Line 10:   }
Line 11: }
```

Line 3 of this program has declaration of a default constructor.

Line 8 is where we have created the object of the class **DefaultConstructor**. As soon as we create the object and write **DefaultConstructor()**, it will implicitly call the default constructor of the class. In this case, the constructor written on Line 3 will get executed.

Hence, we can say that every class has a default constructor and we just must provide the definition of that constructor while designing the class.

Parameterized constructor

The constructor with parameters is called a parameterized constructor. This is also known as constructor overloading. A constructor that is not identical but different in number of parameters, type of parameters, and sequence of parameters can be declared. We overload the constructor for different purposes and initialize the things based on the parameter or input received.

Here, we will see in *Example 3.1*, how to create a parameterized constructor with different method signature:

Example 3.1: Create parameterized constructor with different method signature:

```
public class Car {
  Car() { //Default constructor
```

```
    System.out.println("default constructor");
  }
  Car(int types) { //constructor with an integer parameter
    System.out.println("constructor with an integer parameter");
  }
  Car(String model) { //constructor with a string parameter
    System.out.println("constructor with a string parameter");
  }
  Car(float milage) { //constructor with a float parameter
    System.out.println("constructor with a float parameter");
  }
  Car(String model, int tyres) { //constructor with two parameters sting
and integer
    System.out.println("constructor with two parameters sting and
integer");
  }
  Car(int types, String model) { //constructor with two parameters
integer and string
    System.out.println("constructor with two parameters integer and
string");
  }
  public static void main(String[] args) {
    Car car = new Car();
    new Car(2);
    new Car("Porsche");
    new Car(3.4f);
    new Car("Maruti", 4);
    new Car(6, "Honda");
  }
}
```

Every constructor here is unique since their method signature is different. A constructor or method can be treated as identical when their method signature (argument type, number of arguments, and sequence of arguments) is the same and placed in the same order.

More on constructor

A constructor gets called from base to derive. It means, constructor from super class gets called first and then the constructor from child classes. We will discuss super and child class concepts in detail in the upcoming chapter. Let us understand this through the following sample program:

Example 3.2: Inheritance in constructor:

```
public class GrandchildClass extends ChildClass {
  GrandchildClass() {
    System.out.println("Constructor from grandchild class.");
  }

  public static void main(String[] args) {
    GrandchildClass cp = new GrandchildClass();

  }
}

class ChildClass extends ParentClass {
  ChildClass() {
    System.out.println("Constructor from child class.");
  }
}

class ParentClass {
  ParentClass() {
    System.out.println("Constructor from parent class.");
  }
}
```

Output of this program:

```
Constructor from parent class.
Constructor from child class.
Constructor from grandchild class.
```

Explanation: A program always start its execution from the main method. When execution reaches inside the main method of the program, the very first step of that method is to create an object of **`GrandchildClass`**. This statement triggers the call to default constructor and finds a default constructor in the class **GrandchildClass**. Also, the class **GrandchildClass** is inherited from another class **ChildClass**. Then after, the program will move to **ChildClass** and finds if any constructor is defined under that **ChildClass**. It finds that there is a constructor and this class is inherited from a class called **ParentClass**. The cursor of the program moves to **ParentClass** and finds a constructor. Since **ParentClass** is not inherited from any other class, the constructor of **ParentClass** will get executed and prints the first line of output "**Constructor from parent class**." Later, it will execute the **ChildClass** constructor and prints "**Constructor from child class**." After this, it reaches the actual class from where the execution started and executes the **GrandchildClass** constructor and prints "**Constructor from grandchild class**."

Does something ring a bell as to why this is happening, how one constructor keeps calling the constructor from their super class? This is all because of the **super()** keyword.

Let us discuss the super method in detail.

super

The **super** keyword is used to call the constructor from a super class. When we declare any constructor, the very first statement of that constructor is **super()**. Whether we write it or not, this is how the constructor is designed. The compiler will automatically consider the first statement of constructor **super()**. We can add explicitly as well. This **super()** will call the default constructor (a constructor with no argument) from the super class.

The **super()** keyword should always be the first statement of the constructor. If you try to write **super()** as second and later add statement inside the constructor, the compiler will throw an error "**Constructor call must be the first statement in a constructor.**"

You cannot call a private constructor using the super keyword. Using super, you can call only protected and public defined constructors. If you don't write any access specifier while declaring the constructor, by default the visibility of that constructor will be public.

Example: 3.3 Use of super keyword

```
public class SuperMethodEx extends SuperClass {
  public SuperMethodEx() {
    super("Jorvee");
  }

  public static void main(String[] args) {
```

```
    SuperMethodEx superMethodEx = new SuperMethodEx();
  }
}

class SuperClass {

  SuperClass(String name) {
    System.out.println("This constructor received name argument " +
name);
  }
}
```

Output:

```
This constructor received name argument Jorvee
```

What will happen if we don't have any default constructor in super class but have a parameterized constructor? In this case, how we will call the parameterized constructor of super class?

If there is no default constructor in the super/parent class, then nothing will get executed and there will be no error. The compiler will just check and skip to the next step. But in the parameterized constructor scenario, the programmer must explicitly call that super class parameterized constructor using the same super method with the exact number of parameters and order of parameters. If we do not call that explicitly, then the compiler will generate compile time error "**`Implicit super constructor SuperClass() is undefined. Must explicitly invoke another constructor`**".

Let's understand this with an example.

In this program, we have two classes - one is **`SuperMethodEx`** and another is **`SuperClass`**. **`SuperClass`** is the parent class of the **`SuperMethodEx`** class.

Both the classes have a constructor. **`SuperClass`** has a parameterized constructor, which is expecting an argument string to be called. On the other hand, **`SuperMethodEx`** has a default constructor.

Question: Look at the program carefully and predict the output or error and what will cause the issue?

```
Line 1: public class SuperMethodEx extends SuperClass{
Line 2:   public SuperMethodEx() {
Line 3:
Line 4:   }
```

```
Line 5:
Line 6:   public static void main(String[] args) {
Line 7:     SuperMethodEx superMethodEx = new SuperMethodEx();
Line 8:
Line 9:   }
Line 10: }
Line 11:
Line 12: class SuperClass {
Line 13:
Line 14:   SuperClass(String name) {
Line 15:     System.out.println("You have called ParentClass constructor
with parameter " + name);
Line 16:   }
Line 17: }
```

Clarification: The preceding program will throw compile time exception since there is no default constructor in the parent class, but has a parameterized constructor, which we need to call explicitly.

Line 2 of the program will cause the compile time error.

To fix this compilation error, call the parent class parameterized constructor at Line 3, for example, **`super("You Name");`**

this

The *this* keyword represents the members (for example, variables or methods) from same class. **`this`** works in a similar manner as super keyword. In the constructor, we use the **`this()`** keyword to call or refer a constructor, which is defined within the same class. this should be the first statement of a constructor. If you write **`this()`** as second statement or later, then the system will generate a compilation error.

A class can have any number of constructors and with the help of the **`this()`** keyword, a constructor can communicate with other constructors within the class. this keyword works as a communicator between siblings, which we must use when we want to talk with each other.

Let's understand this keyword with an example.

Example 3.4: Use of this keyword:

```
public class ConstructorThis
{
  ConstructorThis()
```

```
  {
    this(2);
    System.out.println("Default Constructor.");

  }
  ConstructorThis(int i)
  {
    this(2,3);
    System.out.println("Constructor with one argument.");
  }
  ConstructorThis(int i, int j)
  {
    this(2,3,4);
    System.out.println("Constructor with two arguments.");
  }
  ConstructorThis(int i, int j, int k)
  {
    System.out.println("Constructor with three arguments.");
  }

  public static void main(String[] args) {
    ConstructorThis constructorThis = new ConstructorThis();
  }
}
```

Output:

```
Constructor with three arguments.
Constructor with two arguments.
Constructor with one argument.
Default Constructor.
```

Examples of some valid and invalid constructor definition are as follows:

- **Valid constructors**:
    - **Valid syntax**:

```
RecursiveConstructor() {
}
```

- **First statement of constructor**: **Super** and **this** keywords are always the first statement:

```
RecursiveConstructor() {
  this(2);
  System.out.println("Print your message");
}
RecursiveConstructor(int a) {
  super();
  System.out.println("Print your message");
}
```

- **Invalid constructors**:
  - **Super and this at same time**: You cannot write super and this as second statement of a constructor:

```
ConstructorThis()
{

System.out.println("Constructor.");
this(2); //this line of code will throw compilation error.
}
```

OR

```
ConstructorThis()
{

System.out.println("Default Constructor.");
super(2); //this line of code will throw compilation error.
}
```

  - **Super keyword**: You cannot write more than one super within a constructor:

```
public SuperMethodEx() {
  super();
  super("Jorvee");
}
```

  - **Private constructor**: You cannot call a private constructor defined in the parent class:

```
public class SuperMethodEx extends SuperClass {
```

```
  public SuperMethodEx() {
    super("Jorvee");
  }

  public static void main(String[] args) {
    SuperMethodEx superMethodEx = new SuperMethodEx();

  }
}

class SuperClass {
  private SuperClass(String name) {
    System.out.println("This constructor received name
argument " + name);
  }
}
```

- **Constructor with return type**: You cannot write the return type with a constructor:

```
  public String Car() { // this will become general Java
method.
    System.out.println("default constructor");

  }
  public String Car() {
    System.out.println("default constructor");
    return "String";
  }
```

- **Identical constructors**: You cannot declare and define two or more constructors with the same method signature. This is confusing for processor at run time regarding, which constructor to be called:

```
  ConstructorThis(int i, int j)  { }
  ConstructorThis(int i, int j)  { }
```

- **Recursive constructor**: Recursive calling is not possible. It will throw compilation error "Recursive constructor invocation" shown as follows:

```
Public class RecursiveConstructor {
RecursiveConstructor() {
```

```
        this(2);
      }
      RecursiveConstructor(int a) {
        this();
      }
    }
```

OR

```
    RecursiveConstructor() {
        this();
      }
```

Conclusion

Constructor is used to inject the dependencies or prerequisites of a class and initialize the member variable of a class. Every class has a default constructor. We just need to provide definition of that default constructor.

In the next chapter, we will discuss the static keyword and all different approaches to use keyword static with class, method, and variable. Static is a very powerful keyword and plays a vital role in the execution of our program.

Points to remember

- Two or more identical constructors are not allowed in a single class.
- Parameter is also known as an argument. For example, the number of parameters could be referring to a number of arguments.
- A constructor can call only one parent class constructor. By default, it will call a default constructor. When you explicitly call ***super()*** as the first statement of a constructor, then again, it will call the default constructor. If you explicitly call the ***super*** with argument, then it will call parameterized constructor with a matching argument and will not execute default constructor from the parent class.
- The first statement of a constructor will be always be ***super()*** or ***this()***.
- Recursive constructor invocation is not possible in Java; it will throw compilation error.

Multiple choice questions

1. **Which keyword is used to call a constructor from other constructors of the same class?**
   a. super
   b. this
   c. extend
   d. constructor
2. **Which keyword is use to call a constructor define in the super class?**
   a. super
   b. this
   c. extend
   d. constructor
3. **A class can have more than one identical constructor.**
   a. True
   b. False
4. **What all access specifiers are allowed with constructor?**
   a. public, private
   b. protected, final, public
   c. static, public
   d. private, protected, public

Answers

1. **b**
2. **a**
3. **b**
4. **d**

Questions

1. What is constructor?
2. What is constructor overloading?

3. What is super keyword and why do we need this?
4. Why we don't put any return type with a constructor?
5. Predict the output of following program:

```
public class SuperMethodEx extends SuperClass {
  public SuperMethodEx() {
    super();
    super("Jorvee");
  }

  public static void main(String[] args) {
    SuperMethodEx superMethodEx = new SuperMethodEx();

  }
}

class SuperClass {
  SuperClass(){
    System.out.println("rashid");
  }
  SuperClass(String name) {
    System.out.println("This constructor received name argument "
+ name);
  }
}
```

6. What is the difference between super() and this()?

Exercise

Exercise 1: Create a class with two constructors and use this keyword to call constructor.

1. Create a class Human having main method.
2. Create two parameterized constructors; keep one constructor default, and another constructor with a string argument.
3. Create main method in Human class and create object of Human class under main method.

4. Call parameterized constructor from the default constructor with the help of this keyword.

Exercise 2: Create two classes Human and Heart. Both class should have default constructor. Use the `super()` keyword to invoke the constructor of parent class.

1. Create two classes Human and Heart. Declare Human class public and Heart class protected. Inherit class Heart to Human class.
2. Create constructors in both classes.
3. Create the main method in the Human class and create an object of Human class under the main method.
4. Invoke the constructor of Heart class using the super keyword.
5. Execute the program.

Key terms

- **Method signature**: The parameter that we pass in the method is known as the method signature.
- **Access specifier**: Access specifier is also known as visibility specifier, which tells the compiler this particular method or class is visible till this scope.

CHAPTER 5
Static Keyword

Static is a keyword in Java and other programming languages. It is a very powerful keyword, and we can use it as a modifier with variable, class, method, and block. In this chapter, we will discuss the use of static in a different form in java program with examples.

Structure

In this chapter, we will discuss the following topics:

- Static keyword
- Static variable
- Static method
- Static block
- Static class
- Main method

Objectives

After successfully completion of this chapter, you will be able to:

- Understand the static keyword, static method, and static variable
- Understand the role of static with class and block of code
- Explain why we declare main method of a class static

Static keyword

Anything we declare in a program using static will directly associate with class and get loaded when class loader loads the class in the memory. Also, all the static declared things, that is, static members from a class get executed first. As a result of this, we declare main method as static. Class, variable, method, and initialization block declared using static is known and static member of class. Static member of a class can be accessed without creating the object or instance of that class. We can directly access the static member with class name.

Before Java 6, we could execute a program using static block as well. But after Java 6, Java has changed the design and execution of a program and always starts from main method, which is also a static method although static declared things get loaded on the memory at the time of class load.

Class loader reads and loads the class from top to bottom. Hence, static members such as block, method, and variable also get loaded and executed in the same manner as they appear in the program from top to bottom. Two static members written on the class will get executed in sequence. Members from line 1 will get executed first, then members from line number 2 get executed.

Static members are used to make our program and application memory efficient. We use static member to refer to the common properties, which will remain same for all instances of the classes.

Let's discuss the static members in detail.

Static variable

Static variable is also known as the class variable. Static variable gets loaded in the memory at the time the class gets loaded in the JVM. There is only one copy created for static variable and all instances of that class share the same copy of variable. If we update the value of a static variable, it gets updated for all the instances of class. The static variable can be overridden any number of times. We can access a static variable with the name of class, without creating the object of a class. Let's understand the static variable with an example.

Example 5.1: Static variable example

```
public class StaticMember extends StaticBase{
```

```
  static int score = 4 ;
  public static void main(String arg[]) {
    StaticMember staticMember = new StaticMember();
    System.out.println("Static variable without class and object
reference: " +score);
    System.out.println("Static variable accessed with the help of object
of class: " +staticMember.score);
    score = 6; // updated the value of score variable to 6.
    StaticMember staticMemberTwo = new StaticMember();
    System.out.println("Static variable without class and object
reference: " +score);
    System.out.println("Static variable accessed with the help of object
of class: " +staticMemberTwo.score);

  }
}

class StaticBase {
  StaticBase() {
    System.out.println("Value of static variable score in base class: "
+StaticMember.score);
  }
}
```

Output:

```
Value of static variable score in base class: 4
Static variable without class and object reference: 4
Static variable accessed with the help of object of class: 4
Value of static variable score in base class: 6
Static variable without class and object reference: 6
Static variable accessed with the help of object of class: 6
```

Static method

The static method is used to deal with the common functionality of a class. The static method cannot be overridden. It means the definition given in the static method will never change and no class and object can change the definition of static method. It may also be created to share the common functionality between the instances of the class or for any operation the class needs to perform before the creation of object/instance of that class. Syntax to declare a static method is as follows:

```
<modifier> static <return type><methodName> () { }
```

The static method can only access the static variable. Non-static variables are not allowed inside the static method. We cannot declare a static variable inside the **`static`** method, but we can declare the general variable and final variable inside the static method:

Example 5.2: An example of static method:

```
public class StaticMem {
  static int countryCode;
  static void staticMethod() {
    countryCode = 23;
    final String name = "India";
    String lastName = "AA";
    System.out.println(lastName);
  }
  public static void main(String[] args) {
    staticMethod();
  }

}
```

Output:

```
AA
```

Static block

The static block is something we declare and write in our program to load the prerequisites and dependencies. The static block does not have any name. We just use the static keyword and then after block **{ }**. The declaration of a static block is as follows:

```
static {
  //write something here
}
```

Let us understand with a scenario. We have written some function in our program, which is already available in any core Java library and our program needs to get executed. We write these things in the static block and ensure that the required library class is loaded in memory at the time class gets loaded in the JVM. Many Java built-in libraries and classes have been implemented this way.

Here's an example of a static block to print a message:

Example 5.3: To print a message using static block:

```
public class StaticMember {
  static {
    System.out.println("Static block");
  }
  public static void main(String arg[]) {

  }
}
```

Output:

```
Static block
```

We cannot declare a static variable and method inside the static block. But we could use the static block to initialize static variable. Let do an exercise and understand the static block in program.

Example 5.4: Static members inside the static block:

```
public class StaticMember {
  static int rem ;
  static {
    rem = 3;
  }
  public static void main(String arg[]) {
    System.out.println(StaticMember.rem);
  }
}
```

Output:

```
3
```

Also, we cannot access a non-static variable inside the static block. The static block cannot be nested, which means we cannot create one static block inside another static block. Let's practice another example to use non-static variable inside static block.

Example 5.5: Non-static variable inside static block:

```
  int countryCode;
```

```
  static {
    countryCode = 91; //Cannot make a static reference to the non-static
field countryCode

    static { // this is illegal, we cannot create nested static
      System.out.println("Static block inside static");
    }
  }
```

In the preceding example, the program will not execute and throw compilation error. The variable **countryCode** is non-static and we are trying to access the non-static variable inside the static block. Also, we have created nested static block here, which is illegal.

Static class

The static class is a class that can be accessible to another class without creating object/instance of that class. We cannot create a static outer class, or you may say that, there is no static class term in Java. But we have static nested class, and we may make inner classes as static. A static nested class cannot invoke non-static members of an instance of the class. The static-nested class can be accessed without creating the instance of outer class: Below is an example of static class, run this class in your machine and experience the difference between static and non-static class.

Example 5.6: The static inner class and instance creation:

```
public class StaticClassEx {
  static class InnerClass {
  }
  class InnerNoStatic {
  }
  public static void main(String[] args) {
    InnerNoStatic noStatic = new InnerNoStatic(); // No enclosing
instance of type StaticClassEx is accessible. Must qualify the
allocation with an enclosing instance of type StaticClassEx (e.g. x.new
A() where x is an instance of StaticClassEx).
    InnerClass innerClass = new InnerClass();
  }
}
```

Explanation: In the preceding example, we have seen that we could create instance of static inner class **InnerClass** without help/reference of outer class. But, in the same way, if we try to create an instance of non-static inner class **InnerNoStatic**, then the compiler generates an error. To fix this compilation error, we must update the logic, for instance, creation for non-static member. First, we have created the instance of outer class **StaticClassEx**. Then, with reference to that outer class, create the instance of inner class:

```
StaticClassEx staticClassEx = new StaticClassEx();
InnerNoStatic noStatic = staticClassEx.new InnerNoStatic();
```

Main method

Execution of a program always start from main method. It is compulsory for every Java program to have a main method to identify the execution point and start the execution of a program or application process. The main method is the entry point of Java program execution, and will subsequently invoke the other statements, methods, and classes based on application/program requirement. The syntax of the main method is fixed with this signature:

```
public static void main(String[] args)
```

The access modifier of the main method will be always public along with the static keyword. You may change the order of both keywords and it could be written like static public or public static; both the orders are valid.

The main method never returns any data, so it will be declaring as void (void represent null and empty).

Then, we have keyword main and in parentheses an argument of the type array. You can give any name to that argument.

For this purpose and to fulfil the requirement, we declare the main method as static so that class loader loads the method in memory and JVM executes it without creating an instance of that class.

We can overload main method, but JVM will execute the main method, which will have single argument of the string type array. The other main methods of class must be called explicitly as we call the static method:

Example 5.7: How the main method works in Java and overrides the main method:

```
public class MultipleMainMethods {

  public static void main(int[] args) {
    System.out.println("Main with Integer argument.");
  }
  public static void main(String[] args) {
```

```
        System.out.println("Main with String argument.");
        int[] arr = {1,2,4};
        main(arr);
    }

}
```

Output:

```
Main with String argument.
Main with Integer argument.
```

Conclusion

Static keyword plays a vital role while designing your application and software. Using static, you could create common things for your entire application or class and all the instances of the class throughout the application access the same static instance to complete the execution. It also very helpful for memory management.

In a class, we could create a static variable, field, method, nested class, inner class, or static block, and all these members can be accessible without instance of the class. In the next chapter, we will discuss the string. The string is a datatype and a class as well. String is powerful and helps us to play with data in Java programming.

Points to remember

- We cannot declare a static method in the inner class.
- We cannot declare a variable static inside the static block.
- Only final variable is legalized inside the static block.
- You may access and call static member just by using their class name. We need not create object of a class to access the static members.
- A class cannot be static unless it is a member of another class.

Multiple choice questions

1. **We can override the main method of class.**
    a. True
    b. False

2. The static block can access non-static member of a class.

a. True

b. False

3. What will be the output of this program?

```
public class StaticVariables {
  public int score;
  static void assignValue() {
    score = 320;
    System.out.println("Current score is: " + score);
  }
  public static void main(String[] args) {
    assignValue();

  }
}
```

a. Compilation error

b. Current score is 320

c. Runtime error

d. 320

Answers

1. a
2. b
3. a

Questions

1. What is a static member?
2. Create a class with a static variable and assign and print that variable in a static method.
3. What is the purpose of creating static block and static nested class?

Key terms

- **Inner class**: A class inside another class, or a class, which is member of another class
- **Nested class**: Multiple classes in a single Java program

Glossary

https://docs.oracle.com/javase/tutorial/java/javaOO/nested.html

CHAPTER 6
String

In Java programming, String is an object, and we may use this as a data type to hold multiple char values one by one. A string can be use in different forms. A string is a powerful data type used to store and manipulate any kind of data. Java provides three String classes to manage the String data. They are String, StringBuilder, and StringBuffer. All three classes are designed for different purposes. In this chapter, we will discuss all these classes in detail.

Structure

In this chapter, we will discuss the following topics:

- String object
    - String literal
- StringBuffer
- StringBuilder

Objectives

After successful completion of this chapter, you will be able to:

- Understand the different forms of String objects

- Understand the difference between String, string buffer, and String Builder
- Understand how JVM creates separate memory to manage the String objects
- Understand the concept of constant pool

String

String is an object in Java, but we may use String as a data type, which stores long text, a bunch of characters, and a group of characters' values within double quotes. The string is immutable. It means once created or assigned, it cannot be changed. String objects are also thread-safe. Immutable objects in Java are thread-safe, and only one thread can access that object at a time, two threads cannot access a String object simultaneously.

The String class is part of the **`java.lang`** package and has 13 constructors and 65 methods. We will discuss the frequently used methods later in this chapter.

String is a very powerful data type to hold any type of data, including escape characters. String overcomes the problem to store multiple characters' values, since char supports only a single character, and we cannot store more than one character in a char type variable. In a String variable, we can put a row of characters. Here is an example to create a String variable:

For example:

```
String text = "This is a string variable declared using the String data
type";
```

We may also declare the String object to store the text data. Using the new keyword, we create an object of a String class. For example:

```
String text = new String("This is a string variable declared using the
String data type");
```

String literal

String literal is the concept of creating a variable without creating an object of the String class. We may simply use the String keyword as a data type and declare a variable as we do in the case of declaring variables using primitive data types. Whenever the compiler finds any String literal in the code, the compiler automatically creates a String object with a string literal value.

Here, we will see some examples of **`String`** literal:

```
String firstName = "Samantha";
```

Here, the compiler will automatically create String object **`firstName`** with the value **`Samantha`**.

All variables and methods get stored directly under the heap memory. Inside the heap, **Java virtual machine (JVM)** creates a separate memory location called String pool to manage the String literals. JVM also makes sure that there are no two or more objects in the memory having the same content. When the compiler encounters a String literal, it checks the String pool to find whether an identical String content/value already exists in the String pool. If a match is found, the reference to the new literal is directed to the existing String, and no new String literal object gets created in the memory. Hence, with respect to memory, we cannot change the value of a literal once its memory gets allocated. This behavior makes String immutable. The String pool always allocates memory for content, and because of that, the String content gets the memory allocation instead of a variable name, and a variable name just holds the reference (address) of the literal value from heap memory. When we try to change the value of a literal, it actually allocates new memory of that value in heap and updates the reference for that variable to a new value. Let us understand with an example.

The following *Figure 6.1* is the graphical representation of memory allocation of these variables:

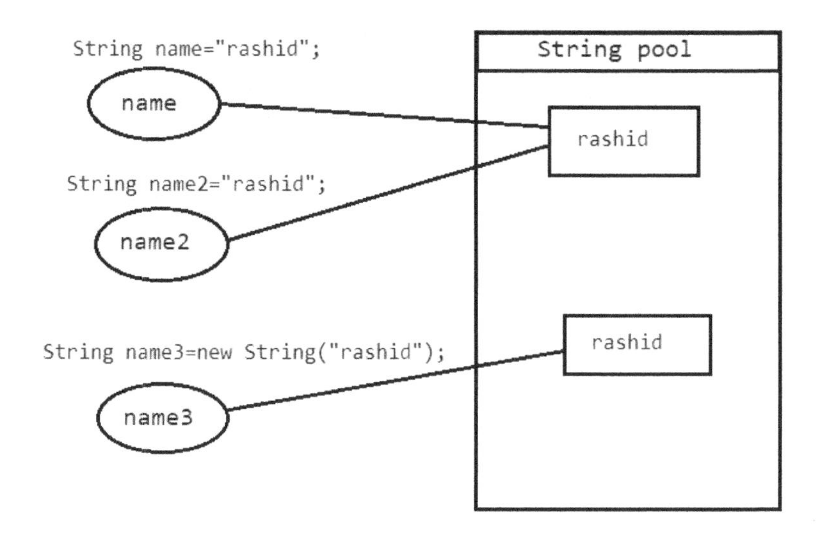

***Figure 6.1**: String pool memory management*

We have created two String literals **`name`** and **`name2`** and assigned the same value **`rashid`** to both the literals. In the first statement of the program, the String name will be executed by the compiler, and the memory of the String value **`rashid`** gets allocated in the String pool since, at that time, there was no content **`rashid`** existing in the String pool. Then, the compiler executes the next String **`name2`** and will find in the String pool whether any identical String value is already present. The compiler finds the **rashid** String is already in the String pool. Instead of allocating new memory for the **name2** String value, it sets the address of an identical String value **rashid** to the **name2** variable. In this case, both **name** and **name2** refer to the same memory address of the value **rashid**.

We have created another object here using the **String** class with the help of the **new** keyword. Every time we create an object using the **new** keyword, that object gets a separate memory allocation in the memory, although it holds the same value. Here, **name3** is the object, which we have created and assigned with the same value, which we assigned to **name** and **name2**. Yet, a separate memory gets allocated for **name3**.

Let's create and understand the preceding scenario with a Java program.

Example 6.1: String pool memory allocation:

```
public class StringPool {

  public static void main(String[] args) {
    String name = "rashid";
    String name2 = "rashid";
    String name3 = new String("rashid");
    System.out.print("Address for both name and name2 are same? ");
    System.out.print(name==name2);
    System.out.print(", and value for both variables is? "+name.
equals(name2));
    System.out.println();
    System.out.print("Address for both name2 and name3 are same? ");
    System.out.print(name2==name3);
    System.out.print(", and value for both variables is? "+name2.
equals(name3));
    System.out.println();
    System.out.print("Address for both name3 and name are same? ");
    System.out.print(name3==name);
    System.out.print(", and value for both variables is? "+name3.
equals(name));
  }
}
```

Output:

```
Address for both name and name2 is the same? true, and value for both
variables are? true
```

```
Address for both name2 and name3 are the same? false, and value for both
variables are? true
Address for both name3 and name are same? false, and value for both
variables are? true
```

In the preceding example, you could see the output of the program. When we compare variables **name** and **name2** using the **==** operator, it is returning **true** because **==** compares the memory address of the variable, as seen in line one of the outputs. In the same way, when we compare **name2** and **name3**, it is returning **false**, because both variables are referring to two different objects' memory addresses. But, when we try to compare the text held by **name2** and **name3** using the **equals()** method, then it is returning **true**, because both variables have the same value, as seen in line 2 of the output.

NOTE: We use the == operator and equals method to check the memory address and string value. The operator == compares not the String value, but it compares the memory address of the variable being referred to. And to compare two String values, we use the equals method in Java.

Methods in the String class

The String class has 13 constructors and 65 methods. Now, we will see a few common methods of the String class.

length()

The method length always returns an integer, which will be the count of characters in each String.

```
e.g. {
String sampleText = "This is the sample copy of title.";
System.out.println(sampleText.length()); }
```

In the preceding code block, we have declared a string literal with the name **sampleText** and assigned a sentence to it. In the next line of code, we have used the length method to identify the length of the given String and printed the result; this will print 33.

isEmpty()

The isEmpty() method always returns the Boolean value **true** if a String is empty; otherwise, **false**:

```
String str="";
System.out.println(str.isEmpty());
```

The preceding print statement will return and print **`true`** because the String **`str`** is empty and doesn't hold any value.

contains(charValue)

The contains(charValue) method always returns Boolean and requires an argument. It would return **`true`** if **`char`** passed in argument is found in the given String:

```
e.g. {
String sampleText = "This is the sample copy of title.";
System.out.println(sampleText.contains("copy")); }
```

In the preceding code snippet, the second line of code will return true because String **`sampleText`** has **"`copy`"** in its value.

equals(Object)

The equals(Object) method returns Boolean and takes an argument to compare the value with the given Strings. In Java, we cannot compare two String values with double equals to (==) operator.

endsWith(String)

The endsWith(String) method returns Boolean and takes an argument of the type char. It will match the last index character of given String with char passed in argument and returns **`true`** if the character is found at the last index of String; otherwise, **`false`**.

```
String word="running";
System.out.println(word.endsWith("g"));
```

Here, the **`print`** statement will print true, since the declared word variable is ending with character **`g`**:

```
System.out.println(word.endsWith("n"));
```

The preceding print statement will print **`false`** since the declared word variable is ending with character **`g`**, not with **`n`**.

> **NOTE: You may use the startWith() method for the string and word starting with a character.e.gword.startWith("r");**

substring(begin) or substring(begin, end)

The substring(begin) or substring(begin, end) method will return String. This String will be a substring of a given String. To create a substring from String, we need to specify the beginning point or the beginning and end index. We have two substring methods in the **`String`** class. One is with a single argument, which only takes the start index of the string and returns the remaining string value after that start index. Another substring method takes two arguments start and end index; in return, it will give the string value, which comes between the given indexes. Let's understand this with an example:

```
String word="Rahul was running that day";
System.out.println(word.substring(18));
```

The preceding substring method will print substring **"`that day`"**. Since we have passed the index number 18 in the substring method, the 18th index will be the starting point and after that, it will print the remaining text of the word.

```
System.out.println(word.substring(10, 17));
```

The preceding substring method will print just text **"`running`"** from the sentence "Rahul was running that day". If you see the argument in the substring method, you will find that this time we have passed two arguments – the first is the start index and the second is the end index. So, the substring will print the characters from index 10 till 17.

split(regex)

The split(regex) method returns Strings and takes regex as an argument. This method is useful to split the sentence and words based on characters:

```
String sentence ="this_isth&new message";
String[] newwords = sentence.split("[&|+| ]");
for(inti=0;i<newwords.length;i++) {
System.out.println(newwords[i]);
}
```

The preceding code snippet can be executed in any Java program. Here, we are splitting the String sentence into words and printing using the system console. We are splitting the sentence based on the different special characters available in the String such as &, +, and ( ) space.

In regex, re has passed [& | + |], character | is a separator for the OR operation.

matches(regex)

The matches(regex) method returns Boolean and takes regex as an argument. It will return true if the given string matches with the given regex pattern; otherwise, false.

```
String regex = "\\w.*";
```

```
String word="this_isth&new message";
System.out.println(word.matches(regex));
```

The preceding snippet of code can be directly pasted in the main method and executed. In the preceding code, we are checking through regex whether the String word has any words or not. In the result, this will give you an output **true**.

Regex explanation: The very first \ is for escape character, **\w** matches any word character (equal to [a-zA-Z0-9_]), and .* matches any character (except for line terminators).

StringBuffer

StringBuffer is like String class, which we used to create the String object to manipulate the string data. We have to explicitly create an object of **StringBuffer** and then only we can store the value in it. The only difference between **String** and **StringBuffer** is that **String** is immutable and **StringBuffer** is mutable, which means we can update the value stored in the **StringBuffer** object. Also, we may declare a String without creating an object just using the String literal, but we cannot declare a **StringBuffer** in that way. **StringBuffer** has **reverse()** and **delete()** methods, which String doesn't have.

StringBuffer is also thread-safe like String, and its methods are synchronized. **StringBuffer** doesn't allow multiple threads to use and manipulate the object; it allows only one thread to use the object and other threads that want to use, will be in the waiting queue and use the object of **StringBuffer** one by one.

The syntax to declare **StringBuffer**:

```
StringBuffer <objectName> = new StringBuffer();
```

The default initial capacity of **StringBuffer** is 16, and it will keep increasing based on your data. We may specify the initial capacity while creating the object of **StringBuffer**:

```
StringBuffer sb = new StringBuffer();
```

Here, the declaration of **StringBuffer** object **sb** will have the default capacity of 16. You may check the capacity of **StringBuffer** using the **capacity()** method:

```
StringBuffer sb = new StringBuffer(10);
```

When we pass the int argument while declaring the object, it will set the capacity of the object. Here, **StringBuffer** is declaring an object with an initial internal storage size of 10 characters. Whenever there is object overflow due to a larger value, **StringBuffer** automatically increases the size and makes it larger to store the characters.

append("string")

The append("string") method is used in **StringBuffer** to put the value at the end of the **StringBuffer object.append()** method, which takes one argument of the type **String**.

insert(start, "String")

The insert(start, "String") method is used to insert any value or data at the specified index, without replacing the existing data. It will insert any data at a specified index and shift the old data after the end of the new data index. This method takes two arguments - the **first** argument is an integer type that specifies the starting index/point to insert the string data and the second argument is the **String** value that we want to store in the object.

reverse()

The reverse() method is used to reverse the String stored in the object. For example, if we would like to read a word from another direction, then the reverse method can be used. For example:

```
String name = "JAVA";
String reverseName = StringBuffer.reverse(name);
```

The preceding line of code will print AVAJ on the console.

delete(start, end)

The delete(start, end) method takes two arguments of the type integer (start and end index value). This method is used to delete the String data from a specified start and end index.

Example 6.2: StringBuffer example:

```
Line 1: public class StringBufferEx {
Line 2:   public static void main(String[] args) {
Line 3:     {
Line 4:       StringBuffer sb = new StringBuffer();
Line 5:       System.out.println(sb.capacity());
Line 6:       sb.append("This is an ");
Line 7:       sb.append("object of ");
Line 8:       sb.append("StringBuffer");
Line 9:       System.out.println(sb);
Line 10:       sb.delete(0, 4);
```

```
Line 11:        sb.insert(0, "That");
Line 12:        System.out.println(sb);
Line 13:        sb.reverse();
Line 14:        System.out.println(sb);
Line 15:        System.out.println(sb.capacity());
Line 16:      }
Line 17:    }
Line 18: }
```

Output:

```
16
This is an object of StringBuffer
That is an object of StringBuffer
reffuBgnirtSfotcejbonasitahT
34
```

In the preceding example of **`StringBuffer`**, in line 4, we are declaring an object **`sb`** of the **`StringBuffer`** class. After declaration in line 5, we are printing the capacity of the object on the console, which prints 16 in output.

Then from lines 6 to 8, we are putting some data into the sb object. In line 9, we have written the statement to print the object **`sb`**, which results in "**`This is an object of StringBuffer`**" as output.

In line 10, we are deleting the characters stored from index 0 to 4, using the **`delete()`** method.

In line 11 of the code, we are inserting the String **"`That`"** at the beginning of the String object. Hence, we have passed the index 0 and String **"`That`"** in the insert method.

Again, in line 12, we are printing the object sb on console, which results in output line 3 **"`That is an object of StringBuffer`"**. Here, you can see the newly inserted value available in place of deleted value.

In line 13 of the code, we have reversed the String data stored in the **`sb`** object, and in the very next line, we have written the statement to print the current value of object sb. In the result, it prints **"`reffuBgnirtSfotcejbonasitahT`"** on the console.

In line 15 of the code, we are again checking and printing the current capacity of the object sb. This will return the current capacity of the object or the number of characters stored in that object, and in return, it prints 34 (which is the number of **`char`** in the object).

StringBuilder

StringBuilder is almost the same as **StringBuffer**, except that StringBuilder is not the thread-safe, and methods are not synchronized. All methods, features, and ways of declaration are the same as we had seen with StringBuffer.

Syntax to declare StringBuilder:

```
StringBuilder <objectName> = new StringBuilder();
```

NOTE: The Java programming language also supports a few special escape sequences for char and String literals: \b (backspace), \t (tab), \n (line feed), \f (form feed), \r (carriage return), \" (double quote), \' (single quote), and \\ (backslash).

Conclusion

To manage and store the String data, Java provides three String classes - String, StringBuffer, and StringBuilder. String literals have a unique identification present in the JVM, which internally creates the object of the String class. We can't create the subclass of these String classes, since these all are final classes. We may store any kind of data or value in String, including special char or escape character. The string is immutable, but StringBuffer and StringBuilder are mutable.

All these classes are designed for different purposes. Based on our needs, we may select the right class to manipulate the string data.

In the next chapter, we will discuss the array and enum datatypes. An array is a collection to store multiple values of the same datatype in a single variable, and enum is used to declare constant variables.

Points to remember

- The String object gets created in the String constant pool. We may create the object of the String class without using the new keyword.
- String and StringBuffer are thread-safe, and their methods are synchronized.
- StringBuffer and StringBuilder are mutable.
- String is immutable.
- Strings have **equals()** and **hashcode()** methods to manipulate the string.
- StringBuffer and StringBuilder have **reverse()** and **delete()** methods.
- We can't create a subclass of String, StringBuffer, and StringBuilder classes.

Multiple choice questions

1. **Which String method is used to compare the text of two Strings?**
    a. substring()
    b. equal()
    c. compareTo()
    d. equals()

2. **The method split() is used to:**
    a. Split the given String based on specified regular expression
    b. Compare two or more String address
    c. Break the String into sub-strings
    d. Delete some part of the string from the given string

3. **Which among the following is not a valid way to declare a StringBuffer? (select multiple answers)**
    a. StringBuffer stringB = new StringBuffer();
    b. String stringB = new StringBuffer();
    c. StringBuffer stringB = new StringBuffer(35);
    d. StringBuffer stringB = “value”;

Answers

1. **d**
2. **a**
3. **b and d**

Questions

1. Write the difference between StringBuilder and StringBuffer?
2. Predict the output of the following program:

```
Public static void main(String args[]) {
StringBuffer sb2 = new StringBuffer();
sb2.append("My name is ");
sb2.insert(11, "Gerard");
System.out.println(sb2);
}
```

3. What append() does?
4. How to make a string uppercase and lowercase?
5. Write a program to match a character and then remove that character from String?

Key terms

- **Thread-safe**: Only one thread can access an object at a time. Once a thread starts accessing, it locks that object and restricts access to other threads. Other threads that try to access the same object will be in the waiting status until the current thread releases the object.
- **Regex**: Regular expression or rational expression is the pattern for search character, number, special character, and string in a copy of the text. **https://regex101.com/** is the best online portal to write and generate the regex.
- **Synchronized**: Synchronized is the term used for the classes and methods that are thread-safe. A synchronized method can only be accessed by one thread at a time. The opposite of synchronized is asynchronous.
- **Thread**: Thread is an executable unit of a process.

References

1. https://docs.oracle.com/javase/tutorial/java/data/strings.html
2. https://docs.oracle.com/javase/8/docs/api/java/lang/String.html
3. https://docs.oracle.com/javase/8/docs/api/java/lang/StringBuilder.html
4. https://docs.oracle.com/javase/8/docs/api/java/util/regex/PatternSyntaxException.html
5. https://docs.oracle.com/javase/tutorial/java/data/buffers.html

CHAPTER 7
Array and Enum

In any programming, there may be instances where a programmer must handle a similar type of data multiple times like a list of objects. Hence, we have arrays in the programming language to handle such lists of data, that is referred by a single name, but can have more than one value.

On the other hand, we have enumeration, which is referred to as Enum to create a fixed list of constant data. This is a powerful variable to declare all the related constants at one place.

In this chapter, we will discuss how to manage and handle lists of a data in Java programming.

Structure

In this chapter, we will discuss the following topics:

- Creating an array
- Purpose and use of Enum

Objectives

After successful completion of this chapter, you will be able to:

- Understand how to create an Array and manage a set of same values using Array
- Understand the operations we can perform on Array
- Learn the advantages of using Array types
- Understand what Enum is and how to use constant with Enum

Array

Array is a collection to store two or more values of same data type in a variable. We can define an array with any primitive data types such as array for int, string, long, double, and char.

Array stores the values based of index number and that index begins from 0. For example, if we store 5 values in an array, then the index of those values will be 0, 1, 2, 3, and 4. Size of an array can be calculated by n-1, where n is the number of elements in array.

Syntax to declare an array:

```
<data type>[] <name of array>
```

Or

```
<data type><name of array>[]
Empty array
String cars[] = null;
Assign values to an array.
cars[0] = "Audi";
cars[1] = "BMW";
```

Array creation and initialization

```
int[] arrayName = {1, 2, 3,  4, 5};
```

Creation of an array with fixed size or length

```
int[] arrayName = new int[5]
```

We initialize an array variable enclosed by curly braces { } and put the values or elements of array separated by comma (,).

We cannot assign an array with contact values after its declaration. So, when we want to assign contact set of values to an array, we must do so at the time of declaration.

Accessing an array

Values stored in an array type variable gets accessed through its index number. And further to add and delete the value in an array, we will perform all using their index number. Let's understand the index of array using an example.

Example:

```
String cityName[] = {"Delhi", "Mumbai", "Kolkata"}; //line 1
cityName[3] = "Chennai" //line 2
System.out.println(cityName[1]); //line 3
```

Let's understand the preceding statements. In line 1, we have created an array **`cityName`** of type string and initialized **`cityName`** with three initial city names as its elements. Cities **`Delhi`**, **`Mumbai`** and **`Kolkata`** are the elements of **`cityName`** array. Delhi is placed at index zero, Mumbai gets stored at index one and Kolkata gets stored at index two. This will form an array of length three.

Delhi	Mumbai	Kolkata	← Elements
0	1	2	← Indices

← Size of Array is 3 →

In line 2, we are adding one more element in array **`cityName`** at fourth place and index number three. Now, since we added one more city name in **`cityName`** array, the number of elements gets increased to four. Now, the question here is what will happen if we write **`cityName[2] = "Chennai"`**? It will replace the element that was there earlier. In our case, it will replace the element Kolkata with Chennai. And new array elements will be **`{"Delhi", "Mumbai", "Chennai"}`**.

Methods in array class

There are many methods in Array class that help us to make the evaluation faster and easier. In this chapter, we will see few examples of methods.

Copying an array

We can copy elements from one array to another, or we may also copy only few elements of an array to another. This is called copy Array in Java programming.

There are two simple ways to perform this task:

1. You can simply assign an array to another array which will copy all the values from that array into the new array.

   ```
   int[] a = {1,3,4,5};
   ```

```
int b[] = a;
```

Another way is by using the copy Array method:

```
int[] c = new int[b.length];
```

Let's understand the copying of an Array with an example:

Example 7.1: Copy array example:

```
public class CopyTwoArrays {

  public static void main(String[] args) {
    int[] a = {9,2,13,6};
    int[] b = {3,5};
    int c[] = a;
    System.out.println("Values of array b. ");
    for(int i=0; i<b.length; i++) {
      System.out.println(c[i]);
    }
    int[] d = new int[c.length];
    System.out.println("Values of array c. ");
      for(int i=0; i<d.length; i++) {
      System.out.println(+c[i]);

    }
  }
}
```

Output:

```
Values of array b.
9
2
Values of array c.
9
2
13
6
```

Enum

Enum is a one of the special data types to declare the list of constants that enable for a variable, which have similar meaning. For example, we create enum to manage the list of months, name of days, and other similar kind of values.

We declare enum with the help of enum keyword and since this holds the constant value, the constraint is to write the value in capital letters.

In a common real-life scenario, we can understand enum such as a short form of code word, which has a meaning. In programming, when we want to hide the actual data from the end users, we prefer to use enums. For example, in our program we want the user to enter a number so that 0 represents Sunday and 7 represents Saturday. But when we are setting the enum for those numbers, we will set with the name of the day instead of sequence 0 or 1, that will be Sunday, Monday, and so on and we further use the same in our program for evaluation. This way, we also mislead the hackers to identify what value is being used in the program and they cannot easily hack the program written using enum. Let's understand this with an example:

Example 7.2: Enum constant example:

```
public enum Day {
    MONDAY, TUESDAY, WEDNESDAY, THURSDAY, FRIDAY, SATURDAY, SUNDAY
}
```

Here, we have declared a enum Day, which holds name of the days.

Now, to access this constant variable in your program:

```
<name of enum>.<constant name>
```

For example, **Day.MONDAY**

```
publicclass EnumImpl {
  public enum Day {
      MONDAY, TUESDAY, WEDNESDAY, THURSDAY, FRIDAY, SATURDAY, SUNDAY
  }
  public static void main(String[] args) {
    System.out.println(Day.MONDAY);
  }
}
```

In the preceding example, we have created an enum Day with set of Days and accessed and printed the first constant **MONDAY** as follows:

Output:

```
MONDAY
```

We may also use the enum contact with values for mathematical formulas or assign a unique value for that constant. And using the getter method, we can access the values of constants. We will see this in detail with an example later in this chapter.

We can also declare a class as type enum, which has a different meaning in Java programming and at the time of compiling, the compiler implicitly adds some additional features to that call. An enum class can have methods and fields. Here is an example.

Example 7.3: The Enum class type example with contacts with values:

```
public enum Day {
SUNDAY(0), MONDAY(1), TUESDAY(2), WEDNESDAY(3), THURSDAY(4), FRIDAY(5),
SATURDAY(6);


  private int dayIndex;
  Day(int name){
    this.dayIndex = name;
  }
  public static void main(String[] args) {
    System.out.println(Day.MONDAY.getDayIndex());
    System.out.println(Day.TUESDAY);
  }
  public int getDayIndex() {
    return dayIndex;
  }
}
```

Output:

```
1
TUESDAY
```

In the preceding example, we have created an enum class **Day**, which has constant methods of day and its explicitly assigned value. For example, **SUNDAY(0)**. Here, Sunday is a constant and its holding value 0.

Later, we have created a constructor, which will help us to read the values assigned in the constant. In case we have more than one value available in the constant, we will create the constructor with the same number of parameters.

In the preceding example, **Day(int name)** is the constructor, which is assigning the constant value to a private variable **dayIndex**.

After this, we have created a **getDayIndex** method, which helps us to get the value of the constant. In the main method, we have written the following statements to get the constant and its values:

```
System.out.println(Day.MONDAY.getDayIndex()); // this line of code will
print the value from constant MONDAY that is 1.
System.out.println(Day.TUESDAY); // this line of code will simply print
constant TUESDAY.
```

NOTE: All enums implicitly extend java.lang.Enum because a class can only extend one parent class in Java.

Conclusion

Arrays are special data types to handle the set of same datatype values, or we say in easy language. Array stores multiple values of the same data type. Every value stored in the array has an address, that is known as index and using that index, we can set and get the value.

Enum is a special data type to create the list the contacts and enum can also be used as a class type.

Points to remember

- The Enum type is only for constants.
- We can store multiple values of same data type in a single array variable.
- Address on array element is known as index. With the help of index, we manipulate a value in an array.

Multiple choice questions

1. **Which among the following is the right approach to declare and assign an array variable?**
   a. String flowers[] = {"Rose","Lily","Sunflower","Tulip"};
   b. String[] flowers = "Rose","Lily","Sunflower","Tulip";
   c. String[] flowers[] = {"Rose","Lily","Sunflower","Tulip"};
   d. int flowers[] = {"Rose","Lily","Sunflower","Tulip"};
   e. String flowers[] = ["Rose","Lily","Sunflower","Tulip"];

2. **Which among the following is the right approach to declare an enum?**
    a. public enum Day {MONDAY, TUESDAY, WEDNESDAY, THURSDAY, FRIDAY, SATURDAY, SUNDAY}
    b. String[] enumflowers = "Rose","Lily","Sunflower","Tulip";
    c. Enum = {JAN, FEB,MAR};
    d. Enum en1=new Enum({CIRCLE, TRIANGLE, SQUARE});
3. **We can declare a class with the enum type.**
    a. True
    b. False

Answers

1. a
2. a
3. a

Questions

1. Create a list of cities using Array and copy first five cities into a new array.
2. Create an enum of months and using switch case, perform some operation for each month.

Key terms

- **Constant**: A value that will remain unchanged or never changes.
- **Array**: Storing same type of multiple data in a single list is called Array.
- **Initialize**: Put or assign a value into an object or variable.

CHAPTER 8
If/else, Case, and Loops

In this chapter, we will learn about conditions and how and why we need conditions in our program. Also, we will see approaches to apply the condition and decision-making process. These are also called control flows of a program.

Control flows are the sections of a code that gets executed in sequence as they appear in the program, but before execution. It checks for the condition and when the given condition becomes true, only then the section of code gets executed.

Here, we will study and practice the use of different control flows of Java programming such as if, if-then, if-then-else, and switch. Using these statements, we manage executing flow of the program and make the decision at runtime regarding what flow is going to be executed next in the program.

We will also learn about loops; loops are statements using the ones we can repeat a block of code several times based on the condition or expression. Until the expression returns true, the loop will keep repeating the execution of that same block of code, which is written in the body of loop. We will see the types of loops available in Java programming and how to implement those in the program.

Structure

In this chapter, we will discuss the following topics:

- If-then-else
- Switch case
- Loops
  - while
  - do-while
  - for

Objectives

After successful completion of this chapter, you will be able to understand the different types of control flows in programming. You will also learn how and when to control the execution of a program. You will be able to explain different types of loops. You will understand the while, do-while, for, enhanced, and nested loops.

If

An if statement is a powerful statement, which we use to decide in a program and execute a code block when the given condition becomes true. This is also called if-then statement.

For example:

```
if(color=="blue") {
system.out.println("Color is blue.");
}
```

The following figure is a graphical representation or flow chart of execution of an if statement program:

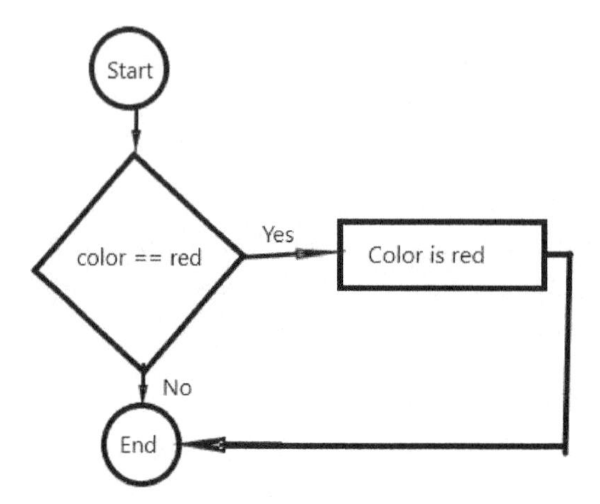

***Figure 8.1**: If statement flow diagram*

IF/ELSE

If the condition which is given in the IF statement is not true, then the block of code that is written inside the if block will not get executed, and to handle the false condition, we write an else statement block of code that gets executed in place of the if statement. This is also called if-then-else statement.

For example:

```
if(color=="red") {
  System.out.println("Color is red.");
} else {
  System.out.println("Color is not red.");
}
```

The following flow chart shows the execution flow of an if-else statement:

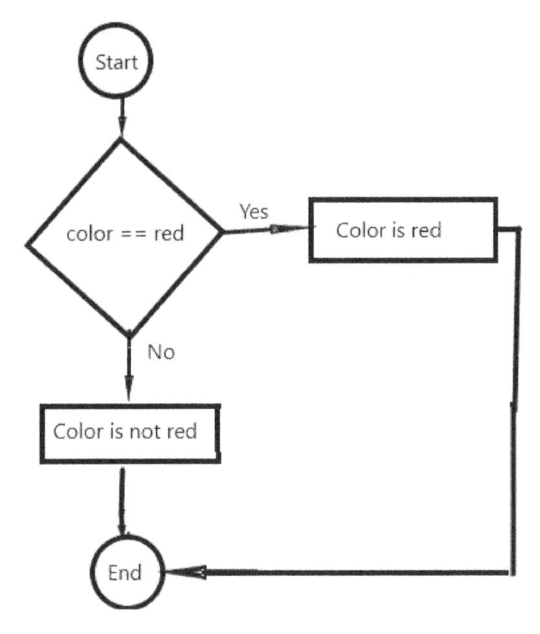

***Figure 8.2**: If-else statement flow diagram*

When a given if condition and expression is true, then program will route to the **Yes** part, or else, it will route to the **No** part of the program.

Nested IF/ELSE

Nested if else is used to perform multiple if-then-else-if conditions in a program. We need this when we must handle or check multiple conditions in a program on same or different patterns. Using the if statement, we can test and compare single value and range of values.

For example:

```
if(marks>= 60) {
system.out.println("You passed with first grade.");
} else if(marks >=45 || marks < 60)  {
system.out.println("You passed with second grade.");
} else if(marks >=33 || marks < 45)  {
system.out.println("You passed with third grade.");
} else {
system.out.println("Sorry, you are fail.");
}
```

Switch case

Switch case is another way of making decisions and executing a block of code written under that case. This is like nested if-else. We use switch keyword to create a **switch** statement in the code and pass a **variable** as an argument:

```
switch(<variable>) { … }
```

In the body of **switch**, we declare cases with possible values to check and a default case to handle the flow if there is no case matched with the given expression. The body of switch statement is called switch block. The following is the example of switch case.

After every case label, it becomes mandatory to write a break statement, which will terminate the enclosing **switch** statement and stop the execution after case label from the switch block. If we do not write the **break** statement, it will execute all the cases from switch block. The break statement is optional and can be used to let the system know where to stop once it starts executing the cases.

For example:

```
String color = red;
switch(color) {
  case "red":
    System.out.println("Color is red.");
    break;
  case "yellow":
    System.out.println("Color is yellow.");
    break;
```

```
default:
  System.out.println("Not matched!");
}
```

While working with any such scenario, where we can use nested if or switch case both for evaluation, then we must think on actual requirements and later, decide the right method. If we are using nested if, then the program will execute all if conditions to find the exact evaluation, but this is not the case of switch. Switch directly jumps to matching case and does not evaluate or check the other cases from the case. So, this way, we make our system faster and navigate to the right block of code instead of checking every condition.

Loops

Loops are the statements that give privilege to repeat a block of code until the given range and conditions are fulfilled. There are four ways to create loop and iterate over a range of values.

while

The while statement is used to iterate/repeat a block of code until the given condition remains true. The while statement returns Boolean value **`true`** or **`false`** after execution of expression. When it returns true, the cursor will go inside the body of the while block and executes the statements. When it returns **`false`**, it will not execute the code from the while block.

Syntax:

```
while(expression/condition) {
statements…
}
```

Example 8.1: while loop example

```
public class WhileLoop {
  public static void main(String[] args) {
    int a = 2;
    while(a<=4) {
      System.out.println("Current value of a is "+a);
      a++;
    }
  }
}
```

Output:

```
Current value of a is 2
Current value of a is 3
Current value of a is 4
```

do while

do while is like the while loop and is used for the same looping purpose. The only difference between while and do while is that in do while, we check the condition later and in while, we check the condition at the first point. The cursor moves inside the do while block and executes the statements written under the do block and later it checks the condition. Hence, the do while block will always execute do part at least once, whether a condition become true or false. And then, it executes the while to check the condition; if the condition returns true, then program will repeat and execute the do statement again and again until it remains true; otherwise, the program will exit.

Syntax:

```
do {
statements…
}while();
```

Example 8.2: do while loop example:

```
public class DoWhileLoop {

  public static void main(String[] args) {
    int a = 2;
    do {
      System.out.println("Current executing index :"+a);
      a++;
    } while(a<=4);
  }
}
```

Output:

```
Current executing index :2
Current executing index :3
Current executing index :4
```

In the preceding program, if we update the condition in while in a way that it will never go to true, even then our program will run successfully and execute the do statement once. Here is an example:

Example 8.3: the do while example:

```
public class DoWhileLoop {

  public static void main(String[] args) {
    int a = 2;
    do {
      System.out.println("Current executing index :"+a);
      a++;
    } while(a<=1);
  }
}
```

Output:

```
Current executing index :2
```

The preceding program will get executed and execute the do statement and block of code written under the do statement. Then at the end, it will check the condition. Since the initial value of variable a was 2, and in the do block, we have increased the value of a with 1, now the value of a is 3. Hence, the condition will become `false`, and this program will no further execute the do statement.

for

For loop is a very clear and an easy way to create loop. In the for loop, we write all three parameters of loop together in a single statement. A for loop statement must have three required parameters and options, and each parameter will be separated by semicolon (;). Those are the following:

- `Initialization`: The beginning point from the range of value. This gets executed once at the beginning of the loop.
- `Termination`: Expression for end point from the range of value, that is, the point the cursor exits from the loop. If we do not specify the termination point in our loop, the loop will enter infinite state and will execute until we stop the program manually or system gets shutdown.
- `Increment`: This expression is invoked after each iteration of the loop and this is responsible to increment or decrement a value of which we are checking in the termination expression.

Syntax of a for loop:

```
for (initialization; termination; increment) {
statements...
}
```

Example 8.4: the for loop example:

```
for(inti=1; i<=5; i++) {
    System.out.println("Value of i "+i);
  }
```

Output:

```
Value of i 1
Value of i 2
Value of i 3
Value of i 4
Value of i 5
```

In the preceding code snippet, we have declared a **`for`** loop, which gets executed five times. We have declared and initialized an integer variable **`i`**.

In the first parameter, we have initialized the variable **`i`** with 1, which means this loop will begin from initial value 1.

In the second parameter, we have defined the termination point **`i<=5`**, which says that this loop will keep executing until the value of **`i`** remain less than or equal to 5.

In the last parameter, we have defined **`i++`**. This expression is to increase the value of **`i`** after each iteration with **`i = i + 1`**. Each time this loop is executed, the value of **`i`** gets increased by 1.

The nested loop

We can also write a for loop inside the body of another for loop statement, which means a loop under another loop. This is called the nested loop. Here is an example of a nested for loop.

Example 8.5: Nested for loops example:

```
for(inti=1; i<=5; i++) {
    System.out.println("Value of i "+i);
    for(int j=1; j<=i; j++) {
      System.out.println("value of j is " +j);
```

```
    }
  }
```

Output:

```
Value of i 1
value of j is 1
Value of i 2
value of j is 1
value of j is 2
Value of i 3
value of j is 1
value of j is 2
value of j is 3
Value of i 4
value of j is 1
value of j is 2
value of j is 3
value of j is 4
Value of i 5
value of j is 1
value of j is 2
value of j is 3
value of j is 4
value of j is 5
```

The preceding code has a for loop inside the body of another **`for`** loop. Here, we will understand the execution process of nested loops. Nested for loops are executed from parent to child; it means each iteration will get executed first from parent to child, then after it will move to parent iteration. Under the parent loop, there are multiple child loops, then execution of all child loop gets completed first before moving to parent loop for next iteration.

In the loop, one we declare the int variable i with initial value 1, at the first iteration, the value of **`i`** is 1. Since the given condition returns true, for loop body is going to get executed. At the very first line of body, we have printed the value of "**`Value of i<current value of variable i>`**". In the second line, it finds a for loop where we have declared an integer **`j`** with initial value 1. But the condition of execution is based on the value of **`i`**, which the program will receive from the parent loop. In this case, the value of **`i`** is also 1. In the child loop body, we have written a statement to print the value of **`j`**. Each time the loop is executed, the statement gets printed on the console. Hence, the child loop gets executed only once and then stops further execution since the condition is not getting fulfilled anymore.

In the second iteration, the value of **i** will become 2 and child loop will get executed twice and the loop will keep executing further. Look at the output of the program carefully. You will find that the number of times the child loop gets executed is matched with the value of **i**.

forEach

foreach is an enhanced version of for loop statement, which can be used to iterate over a collection or array types of data. When we do not know the actual count of data to specify the initial and termination points of the loop, but want to run as many times as the data is present in the given object or variable. This is very easy and clear way to use the loop statement.

Example 8.6: Enhanced loop program example:

```
intnumberOfTimes[] = {1,2,3,4,5};
  for(int temp : numberOfTimes) {
    System.out.println(temp);
  }
```

Output:

```
1
2
3
4
5
```

The preceding example of enhanced for loop is to iterate over an array of the int type **numberOfTimes**. In the **for** loop statement, we will create a temp variable of same datatype on which we are going to iterate, then place a colon and specify the array name **numberOfTimes**. After this, we will close the brackets of **for** loop statement and define the body of the loop using opening and closing curly braces **{ }**. Inside the body, we have written a statement to print the value of temp variable.

We also have another way to write the **forEach**, which can be used only with the list type of data and iterate using lambda expression. We will study lambda expression in detail in the upcoming chapters.

Example 8.3: forEach example:

```
Integer arrayValue[] = {1,2,3,4,5};
```

```
List<Integer> list = new ArrayList<>(Arrays.asList(arrayValue));
list.forEach(listItem-> {
System.out.println(listItem);
});
```

Output:

```
1
2
3
4
5
```

Loops and **forEach** are used to perform the repeated tasks or for executing a set of statements until the condition become false. We use loops when we know the index of an element, and when exactly to stop (that means number of times), so that we can fix the execution. But there are many scenarios when we don't know the index. In that case, we use **forEach** and **forEach** will perform loop operation against each value of the given object.

Conclusion

Java provides if-else, if-then-else and switch to handle the flow of execution of program. These control flows play vital role in making decision and executing a part of program when that condition become true. To handle the false result, it also allows us to write a generic control flow (else or default).

We also have loops to repeat the statement(s) for evaluation or iterate over the collection or array types of data. Each loop has its own advantage and can be used based on the requirement. The while loop can be used to repeat the steps when the condition is fulfilled. Do-while is used when we want to execute the program at least once even when the condition is not fulfilled. The for loop is used to iterate on a range of indexes.

In the next chapter, we will discuss the wrapper classes and generics. Wrapper classes are the classes that help us to create object of a primitive datatype value. Generic is custom class where we give our own definition to a class and its member. Generics helps us to map the data into a custom object type at run-time.

Points to remember

- If-then and if-then-else are the program control flows to handle the execution flow of program.

- Every loop should have three required parameters - initialization, termination and increment/decrement.
- If we do not specify the termination point in a loop, the loop will enter the infinite loop.

Multiple choice questions

1. **Which among the following is not a type of loop?**
    a. for
    b. foreach
    c. while
    d. switch

2. **Which among the following is an incorrect way to declare the for loop?**
    a. for(a=1; a<4; a++) { … }
    b. for(int b=4; b>=2; b--) { … }
    c. forLoop(inti=1;i<=3;i++) { … }
    d. for(;i<=3;i++) { … }

3. **Predict the output of the following program:**

```
public class DoWhileLoop {

  public static void main(String[] args) {
    int a = 2;
    do {
      System.out.println("Current executing index :"+a);
      a++;
    } while(a<3);
  }
}
```

    a. Current executing index: 2
    b. Current executing index: 2
       Current executing index: 3
    c. Current executing index: 3

d. Current executing index: 1

   Current executing index: 2

Answers

1. **d**
2. **c**
3. **a**

Questions

1. Write a program to get the name of a month based on the sequence count of months using switch statement. For example, 1 for January, 2 for February, and so on.
2. What is the difference between while and do-while loop?
3. What are the three required parameters to create a for loop?

Key terms

- **Lambda expression**: Lambda expression is just a shorter way of writing an implementation of a method for later execution.
- **Iterator**: Iterator is the process to read a collection of objects one by one.

CHAPTER 9
Wrapper Classes and Generics

In this chapter, we will learn about wrapper classes, the need and use of wrapper classes. Wrapper classes are an alternative of primitive data types, which we use mostly with collections. Also, we will discuss the conversion of a primitive data type to a wrapper class and vice versa. We will also cover type casting and generics in this chapter where we will discuss the various types of casting, when to perform the casting, and the advantages and disadvantages of type casting.

In Java programming, generics are used to make our code free from the class CastException, which happens at run-time. To prevent the run-time data casting error, we use generics so that the compiler strongly checks the code at runtime and ensures there will be no run-time error occurring related to casting of data. We will see the ways to design generics, including generic class, generic interface, and generic method.

Structure

In this chapter, we will discuss the following topics:

- Wrapper classes
- Type casting
    - Narrowing

  - Widening
- Generics
  - Parameter types
  - Bounded type parameters
  - Generic class
  - Generic interface
  - Generic method

Objectives

This chapter describes about the types of data and their respective data types and wrapper classes. Also, in this chapter, we will demonstrate the casting by changing the data type of a value such as String to char or String to object using the latest Java version with some example programs. We will also cover the generics and type of generics, which we use in Java programming along with out-of-the-box and custom implementation.

Wrapper classes

Wrapper class is class that helps us to create an object of a primitive datatype value. It means when we declare a variable using primitive datatype (int, char, float, and so on), we use the wrapper class of that primitive datatype to create object since we cannot create an object from a primitive datatype.

The following table lists the eight primitive types and their wrapper classes:

Primitive type	Wrapper class
byte	Byte
short	Short
int	Integer
long	Long
float	Float
double	Double
char	Character
boolean	Boolean

***Table 9.1**: Primitive types and wrapper classes*

We need these wrapper classes and their objects while dealing with collection APIs and data structure, where we need to manage primitive data types values. Since primitive type does not belong to any class, to manage the data in collection and data structure, we need to convert those primitive type into objects.

For example:

```
List<Integer> listNumber = new ArrayList<Integer>();
```

We cannot write the preceding statement of code with primitive type instead of wrapper class. It will throw the compile time error **"`Syntax error, insert "Dimensions" to complete ReferenceType`"**.

```
List<int> listNumber = new ArrayList<int>(); // invalid declaration of
List.
```

The preceding line of code will throw the compile time exception.

The primitive type is preferred to perform the arithmetic and conditional operations since primitive type consumes less memory in comparison to the object of a wrapper class. There are two terms that we use to refer these conversions of types.

Autoboxing

When we convert a primitive type and put it into a wrapper class, the compiler auto-converts the primitive type into a wrapper class when needed; that's why this is called autoboxing.

For example:

```
Line 1: public class AutoBoxing {
Line 2: public static void main(String[] args) {
Line 3:     int roll = 1234;
Line 4:     List<Integer> list = new ArrayList<Integer>();
Line 5:     list.add(roll);
Line 6:     System.out.println(list.get(0) instanceof Integer);
Line 7:   }
Line 8: }
```

Output:

```
Problems  Javadoc  Declaration  Console
<terminated> AutoBoxing [Java Application] C:\Program Files\Java\jdk1.8.0_131\bin\javaw.exe (Mar 27, 2021, 10:03:57 AM)
true
```

***Figure 9.1**: Screenshot of output of AutoBoxing program*

The preceding code is an example of autoboxing. In this example, we can add **`int`** type of data into an **`Integer`** class type without error. Line 3 of the code is declaration of an int variable roll, which holds the value **`1234`** (primitive type). In the next Line 4, we have declared a list of type Integer (wrapper class) and created an object **`list`** from that. The list is a member of collection API in Java programming. In Line 5 of the code, we have added our int value into list object. We have written a simple **`list.add(roll)`** statement, but in the backend, the compiler will execute something like this; **`list.add(Integer.valueOf(roll));`**. Hence, this is known as **autoboxing**.

Outboxing

When we explicitly convert a wrapper class object and assign it to a primitive type, it is called **outboxing**.

For example:

```
  long longValue = 12345678912332323241;
  int intValue = longValue; // this line of code generates compilation
error.
```

In the preceding statements, we have two variables; one is a long type and the another is of the type **`int`**. The long type is a big size data type in comparison to int. So, when we try to assign a long value into an int variable, the compiler will generate compile time error "Type mismatch: cannot convert from long to int". But we can explicitly cast that long value into int using a casting. Here in the following line of code, we have casted the long value into an int variable with the help of cast (int):

```
int intValue = (int) longValue;
```

After applying, the cast compiler will successfully compile the code.

Type casting

Type casting is a concept of assigning a type of value into another type. Type casting helps us in memory management, and we need to explicitly type cast when we are assigning a bigger data type value into a small data type. In Java programming, when we try to assign a bigger byte of data type into smaller data type, the compiler will throw compile time error **"`Type mismatch: cannot convert`"**.

Every data type has as a limitation of memory size to hold the value into it. We perform type casting only with primitive data type values:

Data Type	Bit signed
boolean	1 bit
byte	8 bit
short	16 bit
int	32 bit
long	64 bit
float	32 bit
double	64 bit
char	16 bit

***Table 9.2**: Data types and their memory size*

Table 9.1 shows all the primitive data types and its memory size in bits, based on its bit size application allocated memory in the system for a data type to manage or store value into it. We have already discussed these types and their memory in *Chapter 3: Class, Objects, and Variables*. Now, coming to type casting, we will see the ways to perform type casting and how to do this in Java programming. There are two types of casting - narrowing and widening. Let's see these types in detail.

Narrowing

When we assign a high-size data type into a lower size, we need to do narrowing explicitly in our program. Here is the sequence of the primitive data type based on their size in the decreasing order:

double > float > long > int > char > short > byte

For example, when we try to assign a long type of variable into an int type of variable as follows, the JDK will generate compile time error **"`Type mismatch: cannot convert from long to int`"**:

```
long longValue = 1234567891;
  int intValue = longValue;
```

Similarly, we can achieve this when we cast the long value into int while assigning the long value to **`int`**. Here is an example:

```
long longValue = 1234567891;
  int intValue = (int) longValue;
```

You may refer the Program 1 under the Sample program section at the end of this chapter.

Widening

When we assign a small size data type into a high size of data type, it is called widening casting. Widening is automatically handled by the compiler and we need not write any explicit parameter while assigning the value, as we do in case of narrowing casting. In case of widening, the compiler automatically casts that value and doesn't throw any error:

```
int intValue = 1234;
  long longValue = intValue;
```

In case of the preceding variable assignation, the compiler will not throw any error and assignation of the integer value into a long variable will work without any issue. Here is the sequence of primitive data types in the increasing order based on their size:

byte > short > char > int > long > float > double

NOTE: We should do type casting when we are sure that the data which is available in high-size data type will fit in the small-size type; otherwise, the compiler will compress your data to fit into a smaller size of data type and we may lose the actual value. Please investigate Program 2 in the solution program section at the end of this chapter to understand what will happen when we try to compress a big value that doesn't fit in small-size data type.

Generics

Generics are used to make our code type safe and avoid runtime errors or class cast exception from program. Runtime error and exceptions occur mostly when we receive a data of one type that cannot be casted into another type, which is common while working with collections. Generics help us to make our code safe so that we can typecast those data properly as per our need, and the compiler strongly check the generics at the compile time for any possibility of typecasting error and ensures there will be no runtime error or exception. One good reason to use generics is that if any error occurs during runtime, it is difficult to identify the error and fix it. Hence, it is better we use generics and fix those data typecasting issues at the time of compilation. There are three ways to define the generics in Java programming.

Generics ensure that one type of collection will store only specified type of data. If a program tries to insert or add a string data into an integer type of collection, then it will throw a compilation error.

For example:

```
List<Integer> marks = new ArrayList<Integer>();
```

```
marks.add(20);
marks("rashid"); // this line of code will generate error.
```

Line 3 of the code will generate the compilation error "**The method add(Integer) in the type List<Integer> is not applicable for the arguments (String)**" because we are trying to assign a string type of value into an integer type of collection.

Parameter types

A parameter type can be any data type of the POJO class and interface. While creating the object of generic class, we need to explicitly specify the data type or POJO as the type parameter, so that the compiler can run the check to ensure the right type of value is getting assigned. The most used type parameter names are:

E - Element

K - Key

N - Number

T - Type

V - Value

S, U, V, and so on - 2nd, 3rd, 4th types

You will see these parameter names used throughout the Java SE API. These type of parameters can also be array types.

Bounded type parameters

Generic makes the parameter free from any data restriction, but sometimes, we have the requirement to restrict certain types and allow only a type of data, particularly in case of any data manipulation, and our class or method has provision to perform operation only on certain types of data. In this case, we use the bounded type parameter and bound the generic parameter with a data type by using the extends keyword. Let us see an example of the bounded type parameter generic class:

For example:

```
public class BoundedTypeParameter<T extends Number> {

  private T params;

  public T getParams() {
    return params;
```

```
  }

  public void setParams(T params) {
    this.params = params;
  }

  public static void main(String[] args) {
      BoundedTypeParameter<Integer> gen2 = new BoundedTypeParameter<>();
      gen2.setParams(123);
    }
}
```

In the preceding program, we have declared a bounded type parameter. To make a class bounded type, we need to extend the data type to parameter type while declaring the class, interface, or method. In our case, **T** extends **Number**, which means these parameter types only allow the number values **BoundedTypeParameter<T extends Number>**.

When we try to add the following line under the main method of this program, the compiler will generate ;*"Bound mismatch: The type **String** is not a valid substitute for the bounded parameter **<T extends Number>** of the type **BoundedTypeParameter<T>**"* compile time exception. Because we have declared the **BoundedTypeParameter** class as a parameterized class but with a bounded type wrapper class that is **Number**, and in with these statements we are trying to assign a **String** value, into a **Number** data type, which is impossible:

```
BoundedTypeParameter<String> gen1 = new BoundedTypeParameter<>();
gen1.setParams("GenericOne");
```

Generic class

The Generic class is a class that has a parameterized type associated with the class. That type could be a parameter, data type, class, or interface of Java, and can have one or more parameter as type within the angular brackets.

For example:

```
public class GenericsWithTypeParam<T> {
  private T type;

  public T getType() {
    return type;
  }
```

```
  public void setType(T type) {
    this.type = type;
  }

  public static void main(String[] args) {
    GenericsWithTypeParam<String> typeString = new
GenericsWithTypeParam<String>();
    typeString.setType("I am String generic type.");
    System.out.println(typeString.getType());
  }
}
```

The preceding class is declared as a generic class with the type parameter **T**. Generic type **T** refers to a type and that type can be any form of data. In this class, we have created a private variable type of type **T** and created getter and setter methods to set and get the value into or from the type variable.

While creating the object of this generic class, we need to explicitly specify the data type so that the compiler can run the check to ensure the right type of value is getting assigned to the variable. Here, in our case, we have created object with String data type so that only **String** value can be set to type.

NOTE: Please refer to Program 3 and program 4 in solution program section at the end of this chapter to understand some other approaches of generics such as an object without type and multi-type parameters in generic. We can also declare a parameter type as an array in generics.

Generic interface

The Generic interface is declared in the same way as we declare a generic class. The only difference is the declaration keyword **interface**, which we use for interface declaration, and other procedures remain same as we do for the Generic class.

For example:

```
public interface GenericClass<K, V> {
//write your code here
}
```

Generic method

The Generic method is a method that introduces its own type of parameters, which are like the Generic class. We declare the Generic method when we don't want the whole class to be parameterized. Hence, to make a section of class parameterized, we make the method or constructor generic. Here is an example of the Generic method:

```
package generics;

public class GenericMethodEx<T> {
  public static <T> String genericMethod(GenericMethodEx<T> a,
GenericMethodEx<T> b){
    return "First generic is " +a.getParams() +", and second generic is
"+b.getParams();
  }

  private String params;

  public String getParams() {
    return params;
  }

  public void setParams(String params) {
    this.params = params;
  }

  public static void main(String[] args) {
    GenericMethodEx<String> gen1 = new GenericMethodEx<>();
    gen1.setParams("GenericOne");
    GenericMethodEx<String> gen2 = new GenericMethodEx<String>();
    gen2.setParams("GenericTwo");
    System.out.println(genericMethod(gen1, gen2));
  }
}
```

Output:

```
First generic is GenericOne, and second generic is GenericTwo
```

In the preceding class **GenericMethodEx** has a generic method **genericMethod()**. This method has two parameters of type **T** and return **String**. Parameters of the method should also be same as **T** type for successful compilation.

In the main method of the program, we have created two objects **gen1** and **gen2** of **GenericMethodEx** class, which is also parameter type **T** and generic class. Passing these objects as parameters in **genericMethod**, we are executing the generic method.

Best practices for Generic class

- We are not allowed to declare a static generic parameterized member in class or interface. When we try to do so, the compiler will generate compile-time error; Cannot make a static reference to the non-static type **T**.

  For example:

  ```
  public class GenericInterface<T> {
    private static T rollNumber; // This is invalid declaration
    private T rollNumber; // This is valid
  }
  ```

- We cannot declare or create object of type generic using the primitive data type. We must always use the wrapper class of that primitive data type. When we try to do so, the compiler will generate compile-time error; Syntax error, insert "Dimensions" to complete **ReferenceType**.

  For example:

  ```
  GenericInterface<int> generic = new  GenericInterface<int>(); //
  Invalid object
  GenericInterface<Integer> generic = new
  GenericInterface<Integer>(); // Valid object
  ```

- We cannot declare a generic class as Exception class; generics do not have the subclass as exception class. Whenever we try to extend the Exception class to a generic class, it will generate a compile time error. The Generic class **GenericInterface<T>** may not subclass **java.lang.Throwable**.

  For example:

  ```
  public class GenericInterface<T> extends Exception { } // Invalid
  declaration
  ```

Conclusion

Java wrapper classes are classes of primitive data type to create the object of the data types that cannot be used in collections. While working with collection framework, we always use wrapper classes instead of a primitive data type. Type casting is the process of widening and narrowing a type of value from smaller to larger and larger to smaller data type. This process helps us in memory management. Generics is a powerful mechanism to provide free hand to objects to manage the data according to their types. A generic class can be used to store different types of same object, which we decide while creating the object of that generic class, interface, and method.

In the next chapter, we will discuss the concept of **object-oriented programming language** (**OOPS**) and its features that include encapsulation, abstraction, inheritance, overloading, and overriding.

Points to remember

- Type casting is a concept of assigning a type of value into another type.
- We cannot declare a generic parameterized type as a static member.
- Bounded parameterized types are the type that restricts a generic type parameter to a particular data type.
- Wrapper classes are the classes of primitive data type, which we use in collection. With the help of wrapper, we create object of type that is not possible with primitive type.
- Generics are used to make our code type safe and avoid runtime errors or class cast exception from program. We achieve Generics using the Generic class, interface, method and construction.
- There are two type of type casting: narrowing and widening.

Multiple choice questions

1. **Which of these is not a wrapper class?**
   a. Integer
   b. Boolean
   c. Double
   d. Long
2. **Narrowing and widening are the types of generics.**
   a. True
   b. False

3. **Generics are used to prevent the runtime exceptions.**
   a. True
   b. False

4. **Which is the correct way to write parameterized method in generics?**
   a. public static <T> genericMethod(G<T> a, G<T> b){ }
   b. public String genericMethod(G<T> a, G<T> b){ }
   c. public <T> String genericMethod(G<T> a, G<T> b){ }
   d. public static String genericMethod(G<T> a, G<T> b){ }

5. **Which is the correct way to declare a generic class with the bounded type of parameter?**
   a. public class BoundedTypeParameter<T extends Number> { }
   b. public class BoundedTypeParameter<T> { }
   c. public class BoundedTypeParameter<T extends int> { }
   d. public class BoundedTypeParameter<T extends ?> { }

Answers

1. b
2. b
3. a
4. c
5. a

Questions

1. Write the names of all primitive data types and their wrapper classes.
2. Design a generic class of type K and V and store the marks obtained by a student. Calculate the average marks and percentage and print the same in the output.
3. Explain the concept of narrowing in type casting.
4. What is the type parameter? How the bounded type parameter is different from general type parameters?

Key terms

- **Generics**: Generics is a function that helps us to make our code error free.
- **Bounded**: Restricts a generic type parameter.
- **Widening**: Assigns a smaller type of data into a large data type.
- **Narrowing**: Assigns a large data into a small data type.
- **Outboxing**: Assigns a wrapper type into a primitive date type.

Sample programs

Program 1: Assign a long type variable into an int type using type casting.

```
public class LongToInt {
  public static void main(String[] args) {
    long longValue = 1234567891;
    int intValue = (int) longValue;
    System.out.println(intValue);
  }
}
```

Output:

```
123456789
```

Program 2: Reverse type casting with same values and variables.

```
public class LongToInt {

  public static void main(String[] args) {
    int intValue = 1234;
    double doubleValue = intValue;
    System.out.println("Value of int after it gets converted to double:"
+doubleValue);
    long longValue = 12345678912332323241;
    intValue = (int) longValue;
    System.out.println("Long value after converted into int type:"
+intValue);
    longValue = intValue;
    System.out.println("Reverse value from int to long:" +longValue);
  }
}
```

Output:

```
  Value of int after it gets converted to double:1234.0
Long value after converted into int type:-1072736828
Reverse value from int to long:-1072736828
```

Program 3: A simple example of generics with the key value pair of data.

```
package generics;
public class TypeParameters<K, V> {
  private K key;
  private V value;

  public static void main(String[] args) {
    TypeParameters<String, String> typeP = new TypeParameters<String,
String>();
    typeP.setKey("rankOne");
    typeP.setValue("rashid");
    System.out.println(typeP.getValue() + " got the "+typeP.getKey());
  }
  public K getKey() {
    return key;
  }
  public void setKey(K key) {
    this.key = key;
  }
  public V getValue() {
    return value;
  }
  public void setValue(V value) {
    this.value = value;
  }
}
```

Output:

```
  rashid got the rankOne
```

Program 4: Create different types of objects using the same generic class.

```
package generics;

public class TypeParameters<K, V> {
```

```
  private K key;
  private V value;
  public static void main(String[] args) {
    TypeParameters<String, String> typeP = new TypeParameters<String, 
String>();
    TypeParameters<String, Integer> typeB = new TypeParameters<String, 
Integer>();
    typeP.setKey("rankOne");
    typeP.setValue("rashid");
    System.out.println(typeP.getValue() + " got the "+typeP.getKey());
    typeB.setKey("roll number");
    typeB.setValue(123);
    System.out.println(typeB.getKey() + " is "+typeB.getValue());
  }
  public K getKey() {
    return key;
  }
  public void setKey(K key) {
    this.key = key;
  }
  public V getValue() {
    return value;
  }
  public void setValue(V value) {
    this.value = value;
  }
}
```

Output:

```
  rashid got the rankOne
roll number is 123
```

Glossary

1. https://docs.oracle.com/javase/tutorial/java/generics/types.html
2. https://docs.oracle.com/javase/tutorial/java/generics/inheritance.html

CHAPTER 10

Object-oriented Programming (OOPS)

Object-oriented programming (OOPs) is the powerful concept of computer programming, which came into existence with the first object-oriented programming called Simula, which was developed by Kristen Nygaard in year 1967. The concept of object-oriented programming makes the computer programming easy and powerful based on real-world scenarios and has organized the program in data and objects instead of functions and logic object-oriented programming makes our code reusable, scalable, and efficient. Object-oriented programming is based on the principles of encapsulation, abstraction, inheritance, and polymorphism.

In this chapter, we will discuss the principles of object-oriented programming in details with examples and all possible approaches to write the objected-oriented program.

Structure

In this chapter, we will discuss the following topics:

- Encapsulation
- Abstraction
- Interface
- Inheritance

- Method overloading
- Method overriding

Objectives

The objective of this chapter is to give an overview of object-oriented programming. So, as a developer, we should know which feature and approach fits for different situations. We will discuss each topic and class in detail with examples. After successful completion of this chapter, you will be able to understand the concept of object-oriented programming, explain all concepts of object-oriented programming (OOP) and explain encapsulation, abstraction, and inheritance. You will also be able to write and develop code using OOPS and explain the methods of overloading and overriding.

Encapsulation

Encapsulation is the concept of hiding the data, variable, and method from external interaction. We create encapsulation for hiding the members of class by declaring the members as private to restrict other classes from directly interacting with variables. To expose and manage the member variables of an encapsulated class, we need to create public getter and setter for those variables. We mainly use encapsulation to create POJO (Plain Old Java Object). Hiding data lets no other developer know which variable is storing value and how manipulation of that is happening. However, a developer can use getter and setter methods to achieve and use the functionality defined in the encapsulated class.

Let's understand the concept of encapsulation with an example. We have a car that has many features and functionalities to use such as start, stop, play music, change gear and many more. We are just using the trigger to perform the functionality, but we do not know about internal processing and how these things are happening internally. All these features are encapsulated into a single object that we call a car. In the same way, we are developing encapsulation in Java classes, by hiding the actual data and encapsulating everything into a class.

Encapsulation helps us to make the code scalable, flexible, and secure. Here is an example of an encapsulation class:

```
public class EncapsulationEx {
  int score;
  String name;
  float percentage;

  public int getScore() {
```

```
        return score;
    }

    public void setScore(int score) {
        this.score = score;
    }

    public String getName() {
        return name;
    }

    public void setName(String name) {
        this.name = name;
    }

    public float getPercentage() {
        return percentage;
    }

    public void setPercentage(float percentage) {
        this.percentage = percentage;
    }
}
```

In the preceding **EncapsulationEx** class, we have declared three variables and getter and setter for those variables to access those variables for other classes:

```
public class EncapsulationExImpl {
    public static void main(String[] args) {
        EncapsulationEx ee = new EncapsulationEx();
        ee.setName("ABC");
        ee.setPercentage(68.3f);
        ee.setScore(24);
        System.out.println(ee.getName());
        System.out.println(ee.getPercentage());
        System.out.println(ee.getScore());
    }
}
```

Output:

```
Problems  Javadoc  Declaration  Console
<terminated> EncapsulationExImpl (1) [Java Application] C:\Program Files\Java\jdk1.8.0_131\bin\javaw.exe (
ABC
68.3
24
```

Figure 10.1: Output of EncapsulationExImpl class

In the preceding implementation program, we have created the object of POJO class and assigned the value to variables of POJO class using setter method and then fetched the value of those variables using getter methods. The method **`setName()`** is setting value to variable name of **`EncapsulationEx`** class and respectively for other variables. We will discuss more about getter and setter in the upcoming chapters.

Abstraction

Abstraction is a concept of object-oriented programming where we hide the actual implementation and expose only the functionality to be used by outer world or class, which inherits that abstract class. A class can be abstract when we declare that class using the abstract keyword. An abstract class may have abstract and not the abstract method and non-abstract methods can have declaration and definition also. The abstract class can't be initialized, which means we can't create an object of the abstract class, but a class that inherits the abstract class can initialize it. To inherit an abstract class, we need to extend that class using extends keyword and provide definition for all its abstract methods. Here is an example of abstract method declaration:

```
public abstract class AbstractClass {
  abstract int additionaOfTwoNumber();
  void displayName() {
    System.out.println("This is a non-abstract method in abstract
class.");
  }
}
```

In the preceding example, we have declared an **`abstract`** class with name **`AbstractClass`** and have two methods, one is abstract, and another is non-abstract. The abstract method can have declaration only and can't have definition; definition of abstract methods will be given by the class, which inherits the abstract class.

Inheritance

Inheritance is the mechanism to inherit and adhere the properties of other classes, parent, or super class or interface. Inheritance is a powerful concept of object-oriented programming where one class shares the property with other class by developing a relation.

Multiple inheritance is not supported in Java programming because of confusion. Let's understand it this way: Let's say we have a class A, which has three methods **`animal()`**, **`food()`**, and **`speed()`**. Another class B that has 2 methods **`animal()`** and **`life()`**. When a third-class C tries to extend the class A and B and tries to redefine the method **`animal()`**, the compiler will get confused and will be unable to decide which animal method gets called whether from class A or class B.

Java doesn't support multiple inheritance because of ambiguity, but with the help of interface we can achieve the multiple inheritance in Java, which means we cannot extend two classes, but we can implement two or more interfaces into a class.

Polymorphism

Polymorphism is the mechanism to use a method or class in many ways or reuse those classes and methods in a different behavior as required. We implement polymorphism in Java programming using inheritance where a child class inherits the properties of parent class and overrides the methods with their own definition. In simple English, polymorphism means one object use in many forms. There are two ways to implement the polymorphism - method overloading and method overriding.

Method overloading

Method overloading is a powerful concept in Java programming to make the code scalable and reusable. Method overloading is a concept of polymorphism. A Java method which has the same name but different return types and method signature (type and sequence of parameters) is called **method overloading**. In this, we are writing the same method with different return types or parameters of that method and might have different types and the sequence of parameters is different. Here is an example of a method overloading program:

```
public class MethodOverloading {

  public static void main(String[] args) {
    MethodOverloading mo = new MethodOverloading();
    System.out.println(mo.addTwoNumber(4.3F, 88.12F));
```

```
    System.out.println(mo.addTwoNumber(2, 3));
  }

  private int addTwoNumber(int a, int b) {
    return a*b;
  }
  private String addTwoNumber(float a, float b) {
    return "Addition of two float numbers is : " +a*b;
  }
}
```

Output:

```
Problems  @ Javadoc  Declaration  Console
<terminated> MethodOverloading (1) [Java Application] C:\Program Files\Java\jdk1.8.0_131\bin\javaw.exe (M
Addition of two float numbers is : 378.91602
6
```

Figure 10.2: Output of MethodOverloading class

In the preceding program, two methods are defined with the same name, but have a different argument type and return type. Creating a method with the same name but different argument type or return type or sequence of arguments within the same class is called **method overloading**.

Method overriding

Method overriding is the concept of using the same method name with the same type and number of arguments in the sub class or child class. For example, if you declare a method in a parent class and while implementing that method in child class, you give the same arguments and method name for that method, but change the definition of that method as per your need. The @Override annotation instructs the compiler that this method is intended to override the method from the parent class. This annotation helps the compiler to check whether the method is present in superclass at the compile time and generate error if the compiler does not find the method with same name and argument in superclass. This also helps us to make the code error-free. Here is an example of the method overriding program:

```
package oops;
public class Flower {
  public void flowerRose() {
```

```
    System.out.println("I'm Rose. My color is Red.");
  }
  public void flowerName(String name) {
    System.out.println("I'm a flower. My name is "+name +".");
  }
}
```

The child class inherits the **Flower** class, overrides the methods of **Flower** class, and changes the definition. Let's practice this concept with a sample program.

```
package oops;
public class Flora extends Flower{

  public static void main(String[] args) {
    Flora = new Flora();
    flora.flowerName("Marigold");
    flora.flowerRose();
  }

  @Override
  public void flowerName(String name) {
    System.out.println("I'm a flower. My name is "+name +".");
  }

  @Override
  public void flowerRose() {
    System.out.println("I'm Rose. My color is White.");
  }
}
```

Interface

Interface is the complete abstraction that helps us to expose the methods that can be invoked by outer world that derive the interface. As an example, consider a car in an interface and functionalities or features of the car such as start, stop, move, play music, and take turn are the methods declared in the interface. When a sub-class derive car interface, the sub-class can access and invoke super class and give their own definition to that method to invoke the feature of the super class. An interface can contain default method, static method, and constants. An abstract method can't have body (definition) in the interface, but default and static method within interface may have declaration and definition.

Every method declared in the interface is by default abstract and public whether we explicitly declare abstract or not. A class that will implement the interface has to provide definition of all the methods of interface before compilation. If we do not, then it will throw the compile time error (compilation error). An interface cannot be initialized, but only implemented by other classes and extended by other interfaces.

We create interface in Java programming to expose the feature of an object to the external world and third part application and software, and mainly to develop service or **application programming interface** (**APIs**). Here is an example of an interface:

Let's see an interface class of **Car**:

```
package oops;
public interface Car {
  void start();
  int speed();
  default String model() {
    return "This is a luxury car";
  }
}
```

In the preceding example, **Car** is an interface which has three methods; **start** and **speed** are the abstract methods and **model** is a default method. Default method has definition also but start and speed methods have just declaration that terminates with a semicolon. Now, the class that will implement this interface has to give definition of all abstract classes. If we do not, then it will throw the error: **"The type InterfaceExample must implement the inherited abstract method Car.<method name>"**. The **InterfaceExample** is the class that implements interface **Car**:

```
package oops;
public class InterfaceExample implements Car{

  public static void main(String[] args) {
    InterfaceExample interfaceExample = new InterfaceExample();
    interfaceExample.start();
    System.out.println("Your car is running with speed:
"+interfaceExample.speed());
  }
```

```
    @Override
    public void start() {
        System.out.println("Engine has been started.");
    }

    @Override
    public int speed() {
        return 50;
    }
}
```

In the preceding example, the **InterfaceExample** class is a Java class that inherits the interface **Car** and gives definition of all its abstract methods. You may override the default method also if needed, but that is not mandatory, and you can skip and ignore the non-abstract method. If a programmer doesn't want to implement all the abstract methods in the child class, then instead of creating interface, they need to create the abstract class.

Conclusion

In this chapter, we have discussed the various principles of object-oriented programming and how we can use the object-oriented programming mechanism in our software and application development. Encapsulation is for the hiding the data, abstraction is for hiding the implementation, and inheritance is for sharing or inheriting the properties and methods from one class to another. We have also learned about methods and how to reuse and redesign a method using method overloading and overriding.

In the next chapter, we will discuss handling the exception and error in programs and the types of exceptions and errors in detail. We will also discuss how to write custom exceptions and explicitly throw errors and exceptions. We will also discuss the fail safe and fail fast type of programs.

Points to remember

- Encapsulation is a concept of OOPS to hide the data or fields of a class and restrict the direct access of that information for sub class and other Java programs.
- Abstraction is a concept of hiding the implementation of methods from other classes and exposing the functionality.

- Polymorphism is the concept to use a method in a different form. There are two ways to implement the polymorphism - method overloading and overriding.
- A sub-class inherits the functionality of superclass and redefines the method with same name and type and number of parameters, which is already present in the superclass is called method overriding.
- Declaring the method with the same name but different return types, different argument types and number of arguments is called method overloading. This is created within the same class.

Multiple choice questions

1. **Which of the following is not a principle of object-oriented programming?**
    a. Abstraction
    b. Polymorphism
    c. Exception handling
    d. Encapsulation
2. **Which OOPS principle is used to combine methods and attributes into a class?**
    a. Polymorphism
    b. Encapsulation
    c. Inheritance
    d. Abstraction
3. **Which keyword is used to inherit the methods from an interface?**
    a. Extend
    b. Extends
    c. Implement
    d. Implements

Answers

1. c
2. b
3. d

Questions

1. What is object-oriented programming?
2. What are the principles of object-oriented programming?
3. What is the difference with *has-A* and *is-A* relation?
4. Why Java doesn't support multiple inheritance?
5. What is the method signature?

Key terms

- **Super-class**: Superclass is a parent class that shares the property with child class or the class that inherits the parent class.
- **Sub-class**: Subclass is the class that inherits the feature and functionality from another class.
- **Encapsulation**: Hiding data and property from other class.
- **Polymorphism**: Reusing or redefining the same method for a different purpose.
- **Abstraction**: Hiding the actual implementation of the method and class from the inherited class or external world.
- **Inheritance**: Sharing property and data with class after building the relation of child and parent. Subclass can receive the properties of superclass the way an heir receives properties and assets from their parents.

Glossary

1. Java OOPs feature **https://cse.iitkgp.ac.in/~dsamanta/java/index.htm**.
2. Concept of Object-oriented programming | Javadoc **https://docs.oracle.com/javase/tutorial/java/concepts/index.html**.
3. Inheritance in Java | Java document Oracle **https://docs.oracle.com/javase/tutorial/java/concepts/inheritance.html**.

CHAPTER 11
Exception and Error Handling

In this chapter, we will discuss the exception and errors and how to handle different types of exceptions in a program to keep the execution of the program working without any interruption. Exception handling is a unique approach to manage the application and software and take the necessary steps when any data-related issues occur in the program. We will learn about the checked and unchecked exceptions, creating custom or user-defined exceptions, and how to explicitly throw exceptions at certain points.

Let's begin without any delay and learn the concepts of exception handling in Java programming.

Structure

In this chapter, we will discuss the following topics:

- Exception and its types
- Error and its types
- Fail safe and fail fast
- Custom exception handling

Objectives

The objective of this chapter is to understand the concept of exception, error, and handling of exceptions in Java programming. We are going to demonstrate the exception classes and their subclasses and also the operations which may throw an exception with sample programs. Also, we will see how we can handle our program when an exception occurs and write a program that will not generate an error at runtime. After successful completion of this chapter, you will be able to:

- Understand the Exception and create custom exceptions
- Understand all kinds of errors and exceptions
- Write code using try-catch and finally block

Exception

Exception is the event that describes an exceptional condition and occurs on a piece of code in the running program and software that interrupts the normal execution of the program. That unexceptional interruption could happen when a program receives wrong and invalid input data and type of data. When an error occurs in the program, the program creates an object that holds error and exception details of the program such as when did the error occur and what is the cause and state of the error., The program hands over all these answers to the runtime system.

To manage the exception and handle the possible scenarios of errors, we used to write the program in three blocks, try, catch, and finally.

Try-catch

A try block is a block under which we write the code that could generate errors while executing. Try keyword is used to declare a try block. The statements that you want to monitor for an exception are kept under try block. A try block must be followed by either catch or finally block.

Then to handle the error from the try block, we write catch blocks. In the catch block, we write a catch method with an exception type in its argument and then statements under the catch block to perform the action when that type of exception occurs in the program. A catch block cannot be used without a try block. There can be multiple catch blocks after a try block, each handling a different exception type. We can write multiple catch blocks, as much as possible to handle exception classes or multiple exception classes of the same group within a single catch block. In the following syntax section, we can refer to the sample of catch blocks. When an exception occurs in the method or program, the runtime system looks for the appropriate exception handler method to handle the error; that handler is called a **catch block**.

Syntax of try-catch:

```
try {
//statements
}
catch (ExceptionType objectName) {
//statements
}
/*
* Catch block to handle more than one exception class.
*/
catch (ExceptionType objectName | ExceptionType objectName) {
//statements
}
```

Runtime system starts searching for the exception handler (catch block) with the method in which the error occurred and keeps searching through the call stack in the reverse order in which the methods or programs were executed. When an appropriate handler is found, the runtime system delivers the exception to that handler to handle the error; if the system is unable to find an appropriate handler, the runtime system gets terminated.

Exception handling is an advanced mechanism to handle the possible error scenarios and avoid the termination of applications and software. This helps us to print the error message, recover the error, take alternate action when an exception occurs, and prompt the error to users to take the required action.

Finally block

The finally block is a block that we write with try-catch blocks to execute the statements of code that we want to get executed always in all scenarios. Whether the error occurs in the program or not, the finally block of code should always execute. The finally block always executes when our program gets executed; we use this block to write the statements, which we always want to get executed like closing the database connection, closing IO objects, and many others. This helps to release the memory and generate any message for the end-users.

Syntax of finally block:

```
  finally {
    //write your statement here
}
```

The following diagram represents the Exception class and its hierarchy and relation with other classes in programming. There are two types of exceptions - checked and unchecked exceptions:

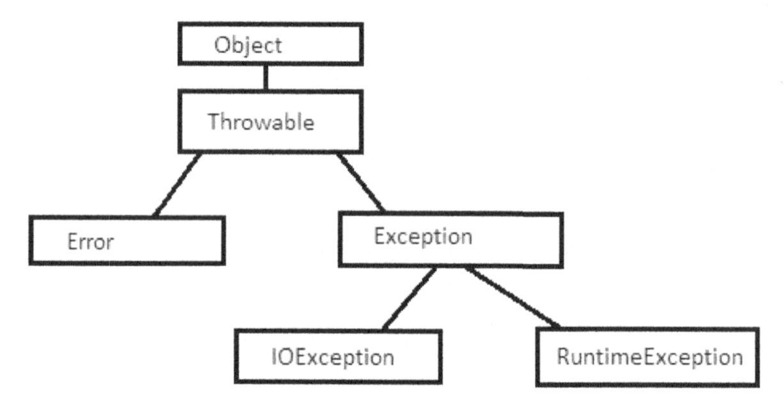

Java Exception hierarchy

***Figure 11.1**: Hierarchy of error and exception classes*

Checked exception

Checked exceptions are the exceptions that the compiler generates at the compilation time. A programmer must handle the checked exceptions while writing the program. These exceptions should be handled using the try-catch block or declared in the exception classes using the throws keyword with the method declaration.

Here are some of the checked exception classes:

- SQLException
- IOException
- ClassNotFoundException
- InvocationTargetException

Unchecked exception

Unchecked exceptions are the exceptions that occur or are thrown during the operation of Java Virtual Machine because of invalid or bad data provided by the user or other applications.

Here are the few popular unchecked exception classes, which are subclasses of the **`RuntimeException`** class:

- NullPointerException
- ArrayIndexOutOfBoundsException
- ArithmeticException
- IllegalArgumentException
- NumberFormatException

Custom exception

A Custom exception is also known as a user-defined exception. It is an exception that a developer creates to define and handle any new type of exception and that is not present out of the box in predefined Exception classes. In Java programming, we may create a custom exception by inheriting the Exception class using extends keyword, and further create methods accordingly.

Let's understand the custom exception with an example:

```
package exceptions;
public class MainClass {

  public static void main(String[] args) {
    try{
      String error = "Exception occurred due to custom exception
triggered.";
      throw new CustomException(error);
    }
    catch(CustomException e) {
      System.out.println(e);
    }
    finally{
      System.out.println("Execution of the exception completed.");
    }
  }
}
/**
 * This class is to define the custom exception class.
 */
class CustomException extends Exception {
  String errmsg;
```

```
  public CustomException(String errorMessage) {
    errmsg = errorMessage;
  }
  public String toString(){
    return "Custom Exception occurred:: " +errmsg;
  }
}
```

Output:

```
Problems  @ Javadoc  Declaration  Console
<terminated> MainClass (1) [Java Application] C:\Program Files\Java\jdk1.8.0_131\bin\javaw.exe (Mar 27, 2021, 3:02:51 PM)
Custom Exception occurred:: Exception occurred due to custom exception triggered.
Execution of the exception completed.
```

***Figure 11.2**: Output of CustomException class*

In the preceding example program, we have declared a **CustomException** class to write a custom exception, which can be later used by the **MainClass** to handle that type of exception. In the **CustomException** class, we have defined a local variable **errmsg** to set the error message, a constructor to assign the message/error received from JVM into a local variable, and a **toString()** method to return the error message for that exception.

Error

An error occurs due to hard linking failure and dynamic linking failure in Java Virtual Machines and these cannot be handled using catch block. These kinds of errors cannot be handled by using exception classes or throwing the exception explicitly.

Try with resources

Try with resources is an advanced way to write the try block. Using try with resources, we can declare one or more object or resource of classes that implement the **AutoClosable** interface and inherits the **Closable** interface, so that after successful or unsuccessful execution of the program those resources will automatically be closed by virtual machine before executing the catch and finally block, and we need not explicitly close those objects in our program.

Syntax:

```
try (FileReader fr = new FileReader()) {
//statements
```

```
}
```

Try with resources feature came in Java 7; before that with previous versions of Java, we used the finally block to explicitly close those resources, which we created in a try block or within the method.

Let's understand this with an example:

```
package exception;
import java.io.File;
import java.io.PrintWriter;

public class TryWithResources {
  public static void main(String[] args) {
    try (PrintWriter writer = new PrintWriter(new File("data.txt"))) {
      writer.print("this is a file written using try with resources.");
    } catch(Exception e) {
      System.out.println(e);
    } finally {
      System.out.println("File writing completed.");
    }
  }
}
```

Output:

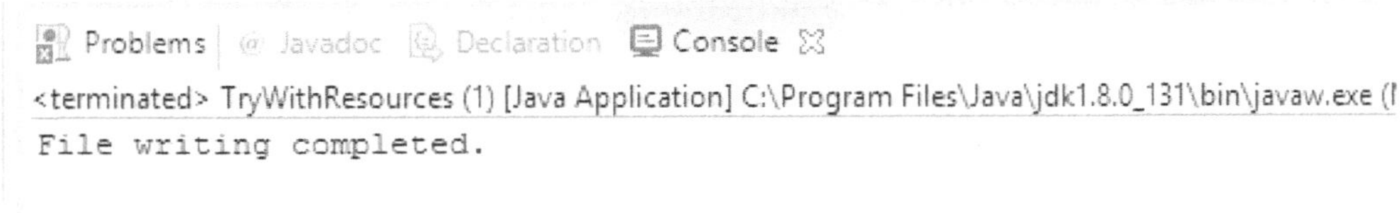

```
Problems  @ Javadoc  Declaration  Console
<terminated> TryWithResources (1) [Java Application] C:\Program Files\Java\jdk1.8.0_131\bin\javaw.exe (
File writing completed.
```

Figure 11.3*: Output of above TryWithResources class*

The preceding sample program is an example of try with resources, where, while writing the try block, before opening the try block, we have declared the resource of Java IO **`PrintWriter`**. This **`PrintWriter`** resource will further use the try block, and after execution, the resource will get closed automatically. We need not explicitly close the object of the **`PrintWriter`** class. This is an advantage of try with resources which is very useful for memory management and garbage collection.

Throwing exception explicitly

In Java programming, we may also throw exceptions explicitly using the throw keyword. This means we can explicitly throw the exception with any statement of the code without any auto-generation error or exception. This will help us trigger the exception on certain checks and perform the action which is required for that.

Conclusion

Exception handling is a powerful and important concept in computer programming to prevent and handle the unexpected behavior of software and application, which includes bad data, bad request, and required data or system is missing or not available. We handle exceptions using try-catch-finally blocks, which are common in all other advanced programming languages such as C#.

We may create our own exception class and use that class further to handle the exceptions according to the requirement using handlers, which is called a custom exception. Handlers are the methods in which we try to resolve the exception or send the pointer back to the last execution step.

In the next chapter, we will discuss the collection framework in Java and the types of collections available in the Java programming language to manage the data or content.

Points to remember

- We create a catch block to handle the exceptions.
- Using the throw keyword, we can explicitly throw the exception at any statement of the program.
- Catch block is the block that handles the exceptions that occur in the try block. A program may have more than one catch block.
- The finally block is the block that we create to execute such kind of exception, which we always want to get executed in the program whether the exception occurs or not.

Multiple choice questions

1. **Which is the right catch statement?**
    a. catch { / / statements }
    b. catch (ExceptionType Ex) { / /Statements }

   c. catch (Exception) { / /statements }
   d. Try-catch() { / /statements }

2. **Is it mandatory to have at least one catch block in try-catch exception handling?**
   a. True
   b. False

Answers

1. **b**
2. **b**

Questions

1. Write a program and handle null pointer exception using try with resources.
2. Why the finally block is important?

Glossary

https://javadoc.scijava.org/Java6/java/lang/RuntimeException.html

CHAPTER 12
Collections

In this chapter, we will discuss the advanced features of Java programming that we use to handle a group of data and manipulate with those data using various Java collection classes and interfaces. In general, collections are a group of objects that can be managed and stored together. Collection is the root level of interface. List, Queue, and Set are the child classes of Collection interface.

Collections are a part of the `java.util` package, which implements the Collection interface and different kinds of data structures to solve the various purposes of data storage.

Structure

In this chapter, we will cover advanced feature of Java programming, the collection framework:

- List
    - ArrayList
    - Vector
- Queue
    - PriorityQueue

    - LinkedList
- Set
    - HashSet
    - LinkedHashSet
    - TreeSet
- Map
    - HashMap
    - LinkedHashMap
    - TreeMap

Objectives

After successfully completing this chapter, you will be able to understand and explain the collection framework, which helps us to deal with different groups of objects. You will also learn about the collection interface that provides the methods to perform various operations on the objects. In this chapter, we will also look at the types of collections and discuss each type of collection in detail with their implementation and sample programs. We do not actually use the collection interfaces directly for implementation, but the implementation happens using their sub classes, we will also be covered in this chapter. Let us start the journey of collections from here.

Collection

Collection is a framework of predefined classes and interfaces that Java provides to manage the group of objects. Collection is an extension of Array and has interfaces like List, Queue, and Set. With the help of collection, we can group many elements into a single element. In general language, we may consider the collection as a container in which we can put multiple elements together. Here is the hierarchy of interfaces and classes that falls under collection framework:

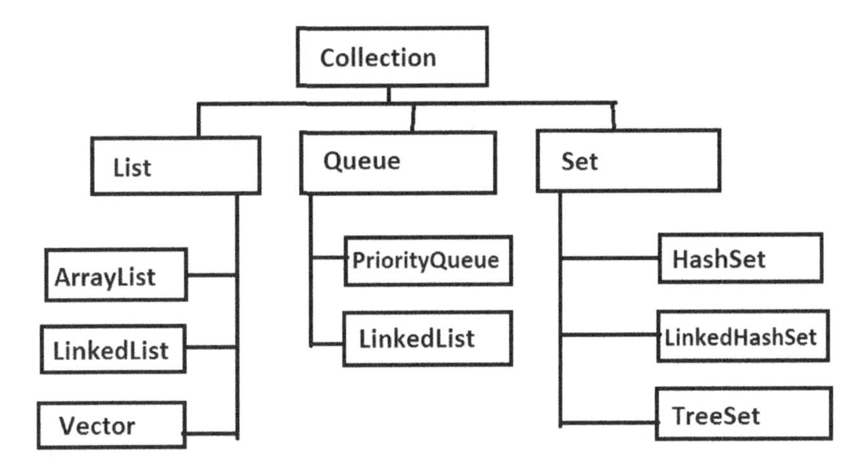

***Figure 12.1**: Hierarchy of interfaces and classes in collection framework*

The Collection framework has mainly three interfaces - List, Queue, and Set and one additional interface Map, which is not inherited from the collection interface. These interfaces are not for direct implementation, but for implementation, we need to use their sub-classes as given in the preceding figure.

Collection classes that are actual implementations of the collection framework use the methods of collection interface. So, all collection classes such as HashMap, HashSet, LinkedList, TreeSet, PriorityQueue use collection methods like **`add()`**, **`contains()`**, **`equals()`**, **`iterator()`**, **`clear()`**, **`remove()`**, **`size()`**, and many more.

List

List is an ordered collection to store a group of objects in a sequence as they are added in the list object. We may access an element from a list from any index using the unique index number. List is an extension of core Array classes and their indexing gets assigned in the same way as it works with an array. The first element of a list will get added at the index of Zero(0) and last element in the list will have the index *n*-1, where n is the number of elements. We can insert, delete and fetch the data on/from any index of list using the index number. A list object can have any number of null elements and duplicate values.

List can be implemented using ArrayList, LinkedList, and Vector. All list classes have some advantages and disadvantages and according to their features, those are recommended or preferred to use or handle the different situations that fit in that solution. Let's discuss the advantages, disadvantages, and features of ArrayList, LinkedList, and Vector.

ArrayList

ArrayList is preferred and used when we want to perform fast access and sorting on the list of data. ArrayList internally uses array to store the data. ArrayList is dynamic and due to this behavior, it grows the size of array automatically when we try to insert elements beyond the declared size. ArrayList also shrinks the size when we remove elements from ArrayList. ArrayList automatically increases and decreases its size by half of the current array list; for example, if we have declared an ArrayList with initial size of 10 and if we try to add 11th element into it, then the size of ArrayList increases automatically to 15.

In case of increase; when we try to push an element in array beyond its defined index, then the size of array automatically increases:

```
Size of ArrayList = n + n/2;
```

In case of decrease; an array will not remove the index until half of the array indexes become empty:

```
Size of ArrayList = n - n/2;
```

Here n = *current size of array.*

A sample program of List interface using ArrayList:

```
import java.util.ArrayList;
public class arrayList {
   public static void main(String[] args)
      {
         ArrayList<String> list = new ArrayList<String>();
         list.add("FIRST");
         list.add("SECOND");
         list.add("THIRD");
         list.add("FOURTH");
         list.add("FIFTH");

         for (int i = 0; i < list.size(); i++) {
            System.out.println(list.get(i));
         }
         System.out.println("Size of array " + list.size());
}
}
```

Output:

```
FIRST
SECOND
THIRD
FOURTH
FIFTH
Size of array 5
```

```
Problems @ Javadoc Declaration Console
<terminated> arrayList [Java Application] C:\Program Files\Java\jdk1.8.0_131\bin\javaw.exe (
FIRST
SECOND
THIRD
FOURTH
FIFTH
Size of array 5
```

***Figure 12.2**: Output of the preceding ArrayList program*

LinkedList

LinkedList is preferred when we want to perform frequent manipulation on list data. Searching with LinkedList is slow and decreases the performance of application. LinkedList has all the similar methods, which ArrayList has, and declaration is also similar like ArrayList. Every element in LinkedList refers as Node and each Node holds two items, the first element value or content and second address or pointer of the next Node. Let's understand the linked list in a graphical form. Here is the example of a singly LinkedList object:

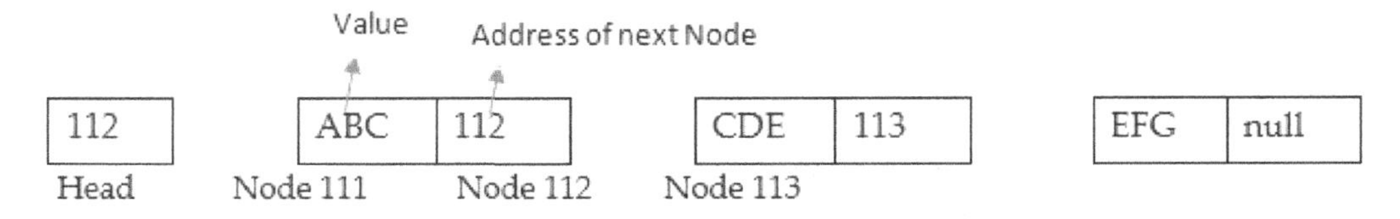

***Figure 12.3**: Example of singly LinkedList object*

NOTE: Head is always the first element of the LinkedList that doesn't hold any value but the address of first Node of the LinkedList.

The last Node of the LinkedList doesn't have a reference or address of next Node, because that is the end of the List; so the address section contains null.

Vector

Vector is a dynamic array that increases and decreases the array size based on the requirement. We can access the vector in the same way as we access the elements from an array or using the unique index number of elements. When we declare a vector with the initial size of 5 and want to insert the 6th element into it, the Vector will automatically double the size of its object. Hence, in this case, after inserting the 6th element, the size of vector grows to 10. Vector is also thread safe and synchronized, which means only one thread can access the vector at a time, and the other thread, which wants to access the same vector object must wait. We will study Thread in detail in *Chapter 14: Thread.*

Queue

Queue is the collection interface or also a data structure, which supports insertion and deletion from both sides of the queue. Queue traditionally maintains the order of **FIFO** (**First In First Out**), that means the element, which is inserted in the queue first will get processed first, but this does not happen in all cases and since we can perform operations from any side (front and rear) of the queue. Hence, an element can be inserted, modified and removed from any side. Queue does not allow insertion of null elements, but some implementations of queue like LinkedList allows the null elements. We can add duplicate elements in the queue.

Like object of List interface, we cannot access the element from the middle or any other index of the element other than first and last. Iteration is only possible in the queue from front and insertion from rear. The following diagram can help us understand the queue:

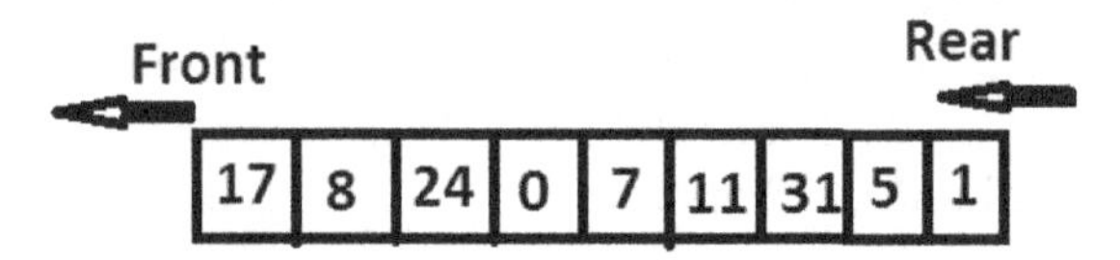

***Figure 12.4**: Elements stored in the Queue*

Front, which is the head side, is used only to fetch and remove elements. Inserting/ adding new elements in the queue always takes place from rear, which is called tail.

There is no direct implementation of Queue; we use sub classes of Queue to implement the Queue in program. There are two types of Queues that can be used in Java programming.

PriorityQueue

PriorityQueue: This is the implementation of queue in which an element is stored in the queue based on the specified comparator. We specify comparator at the time of declaring the PriorityQueue. PriorityQueue is an exception on the basic principle of queue that says queue supports FIFO (first-in first-out) and element in the queue can only be added and removed from beginning or end of the queue. But elements in PriorityQueue can be placed as per the supplied comparator or element's natural order or LIFO as per the requirement. If we don't pass a comparator to instruct the storage term, then PriorityQueue stores the element in its natural order. For example, PriorityQueue will maintain the order 0-9 and A-Z for numbers and characters, respectively.

Whatever may be the order we have provided to the PriorityQueue to store elements, the operation to add and remove elements in the queue can only be from tail and head. Tail is used to add new elements and head to remove the elements from the queue.

LinkedList

LinkedList is also considered as part of Queue. And using the PriorityQueue, we cannot add null elements, but we can with the help of LinkedList.

Operation on Queue

There are two methods to perform each operation on the queue object such as **`add`**, **`remove`**, and **`fetch`**. Here is the summary table of those methods:

Operation	Throws exception when operation fails	Returns special value
Insert	**`add()`**	**`offer()`**
Remove	**`remove()`**	**`poll()`**
Retrieve	**`element()`**	**`peek()`**

***Table 12.1**: Methods on Queue to perform operations*

The preceding table has a list of methods to perform the operation with queue objects. Each operation has two methods, one will throw the exception when the action is not possible on the queue, and the other method will return null/false without any error or exception. For example, **`add`** and **`offer`** are the two methods to insert elements in the queue. The only difference between these two methods is the **`add()`** method throws an unchecked exception when action is not possible or fails to add an element in the queue, but the **offer()** method returns false when operation is not possible on the object of the queue.

Removal of an element is only possible from the head of the queue. For that, we have two methods **poll()** and **remove()**. These methods will fetch and remove the first element from the head of the queue. The only difference between the **poll()** and **remove()** method is **remove()** throws an exception if the queue is empty and **poll()** returns null if the queue is empty.

Also, there are two methods to get the elements from a queue. They are **element()** and **peek()**. The difference between the **element()** and **peek()** methods is **element()** throws an exception if the queue is empty and **peek()** returns null if the queue is empty.

Set

Set is a collection interface that does not allow duplicate elements. A set object can allow only one null element. Set is used to create a collection of unique objects and maintain the uniqueness. When we try to insert an element that is already present in the set, then instead of creating new object Set will replace the element, which has same value in the object.

Set is not like other collection interfaces like Lists where we can access any random element from the object. Random access of any element is not possible in Set.

There are three main types of Sets - HashSet, LinkedHashSet, and TreeSet; these are the actual implementation of the Set and have some unique and different features from each other. Let's discuss all types of Sets in detail.

HashSet

The HashSet class maintains uniqueness of data and does not store duplicate element, but HashSet allows to store a null element. HashSet internally uses and stores elements in HashTable, which is a part of HashMap. HashTable stores elements in the pair of key and value. When we create an object of HashSet, a HashMap object automatically gets created along with the HashSet to store the data elements. We will discuss more on HashTable and HashMap later in this chapter.

When we add an element in the HashSet, that element will get added as a key in HashTable, and to put a dummy value in the place of value. Dummy value gets created automatically by collection as a final object **PRESENT** of Object type and stores as a value for every key. The auto declaration of the **PRESENT** object is as follows:

```
private static final Object PRESENT = new Object();
```

The **PRESENT** constant object is the value for all the keys stored in the HashSet. This will not appear anywhere on the front to the programmer; this is all about managing the storage and data in the memory.

An example of HashSet to create a list of cities:

The following figure shows the pairs of keys and values:

Key	Value
New Delhi	PRESENT
Mumbai	PRESENT
Chennai	PRESENT
Kolkata	PRESENT

***Figure 12.5:** Keys and their values mapped in a HashSet*

We will now look at the HashSet program that will store a list of cities. Let us understand it using a sample Java program:

```
package collectionSet;
import java.util.HashSet;
import java.util.Iterator;

public class HashSetCollection
{
    public static void main(String[] args)
    {
        HashSet<String> cities = new HashSet<String>();
       //  Below line of code will remove element from HashSet
        cities.add("New Delhi");
        cities.add("Mumbai");
        cities.add("Chennai");
        cities.add("Kolkata");
        //Below line of code will remove element from HashSet
        cities.remove("New Delhi");

        Iterator iterator = cities.iterator();
while(iterator.hasNext()) {
  String nameOfCity=(String) iterator.next();
```

```
    System.out.println(nameOfCity);
  }
    }
}
```

Output:

```
Chennai
Kolkata
Mumbai
```

The preceding program has an object cities of the type HashSet. In the cities, we have added the name of four cities as **`New Delhi`**, **`Mumbai`**, **`Chennai`** and **`Kolkata`** using the **`add()`** method. After this, we have removed one element **`"New Delhi"`** using the **`remove()`** method of the collection interface. Later, we have created the object of Iterator class, which will help us to read and retrieve the elements from HashSet and then using the while loop, we have iterated each element of HashSet and printed the value on console.

LinkedHashSet

The **`LinkedHashSet`** class inherits the collection interface that maintains the insertion order of HashSet and internally uses doubly linked list to store the data and manage the structure of data. The difference between HashSet and LinkedHashSet are as follows:

LinkedHashSet orders the elements as they are pushed into the object but HashSet doesn't. Hence, using LinkedHashSet we know and get the fifth number of element that is added at fifth turn and third element at third respectively. But using HashSet, we don't know this order and when we read elements from HashSet, which can be any at any place.

LinkedHashSet is not synchronized and multiple threads can add and remove the objects concurrently, so there are chances of data ambiguity and data mismatch. We can make the object thread safe using the **`synchronized()`** method of the Collections framework. Here is the syntax to make a LinkedHashSet thread safe:

```
Collections.synchronizedSet(new
LinkedHashSet(<NameOfTheLinkedHashSet>));
```

TreeSet

TreeSet is another implementation of the Set interface, which maintains sorting of the data in ascending order. For that, we must specify and supply the comparator while declaring the TreeSet. If we don't supply any comparator, then TreeSet will sort the elements based of the natural ascending order, like 0-9 or A-Z. TreeSet internally uses TreeMap like other Set classes. The cost of the basic operations with TreeSet implementation like add, remove and contains, provides guaranteed *log(n)* time cost.

TreeSet is not synchronized, which means any number of threads can access the TreeSet object at the same time and perform basic operations on the object. To make it thread safe, we must have to explicitly synchronize the object, so that only one thread can be accessed at a time and other threads are kept in waiting state until the operation of one thread has not been completed.

TreeSet object is fail-fast, which means when we try to add element in the TreeSet after creating the iterator, it will generate **`ConcurrentModificationException`** exception, but there will be no exception thrown when we perform operation using its own method like **`remove()`**.

Syntax to declare a TreeSet is as follows:

```
TreeSet<DataType> treeSetObject = new TreeSet< DataType >();
```

An example program of TreeSet implementation:

```
import java.util.TreeSet;

public class TreeSetJavaCollection
{
    public static void main(String[] args)
    {
        TreeSet<String> treeSet = new TreeSet<String>();

        //Adding elements to treeSet
        treeSet.add("A");
        treeSet.add("Z");
        treeSet.add("N");
        treeSet.add("K");
        treeSet.add("B");
        treeSet.add("D");
        treeSet.add("Y");

        System.out.println(treeSet);
    }
}
```

Output:

```
[A, B, D, K, N, Y, Z]
```

The preceding program is the implementation of TreeSet that is declared to store String values into it. Using the **`add()`** method, we have added seven String types of objects into it. Those objects are A, Z, N, K, B, D, and Y.

When we read the TreeSet, we found that TreeSet has stored the object in the natural order of the elements, and we got the output in ascending order of alphabets, that is, A, B, D, K, N, Y, and Z.

Map

Map is an interface that maps keys with values by storing elements in pair of Key and Value. Each key is mapped with a value. An object of Map can hold one null key and multiple null values.

HashMap

HashMap is like Set and stores the elements in the pair of key and value. Each element of the HashMap stores the element in the form of Key and its Value. HashMap can have only one null key, but may have multiple null values. HashMap supports and accepts duplicate elements also as a value only, there will be no duplicate key allowed in the bucket of HashMap. HashMap internally uses **`hashCode()`** and **`equals()`** methods to generate the hashing of the key and places in the Map that helps to make and maintain uniqueness of the key of the HashMap. We will discuss more on these methods later in this chapter. Average time to perform the basic operations like **`get()`** and **`put()`** is constant, that is **`O(1)`**.

Internally, HashMap creates a HashTable with a bucket of initial size 16. When we put a value in HashMap, it will get stored in HashTable. When HashMap reaches the threshold level, then automatically the size of the HashMap increases to double of the current size.

Now after reading this, a question must arise in our mind that how HashMap or system knows when to increase the size of HashMap? The answer for this question is Load Factor. Load factor tells us the ratio of the number of records to the number of addresses within a data structure. In case of HashMap, the default load factor is 0.75f, so when 75 percent of addresses or nodes have been filled with records, it triggers the threshold and increases the size of HashMap.

Threshold is calculated with the help of *current capacity* and load *factor*:

threshold = current capacity * load factor

Initial threshold can be calculated with default sets that is:

Threshold = 16 * 0.75 = 12

In a default HashMap, the size of HashMap increases after putting the 12th element in the HashMap object.

LinkedHashMap

The **LinkedHashMap** class extends HashMap and implements Map interface to add-on more features on **HashMap** class. This implementation places and maintains the insertion order of object. Hence, we can predict at what place we can find a particular object based on the inserted order. Insertion order doesn't get affected if we remove any entries or re-insert an entry into the list. This also stores the entries in the pair of key and value as HashMap does. As we are already aware about the LinkedList data structure, the same applies here also and **LinkedHashMap** uses doubly linked list to manage and store the data.

LinkedHashMap is not synchronized and thread safe, but we can make an object thread safe using the synchronized method of collections interface. If we want to restrict the program and allow only one thread to perform the operation on the object and lock the block of code for the other threads while one thread is performing operation, then we make **LinkedHashMap** object thread safe to overcome the situation of data discrepancies. Here is the syntax of the **synchronizedMap()** method of **Collections** interface to make a LinkedHashMap object thread safe:

```
Collections.synchronizedMap(new
LinkedHashMap(<NameOfTheLinkedHashMap>));
```

A **LinkedHashMap** exactly uses the same initial capacity and load factor as HashMap, that is, initial capacity of 16 and load factor is 0.75. **LinkedHashMap** is fail-fast that means iterators returned by iterator method will get modified by only its own **remove()** method; if we try to put an object, the iterator will throw **ConcurrentModificationException**.

TreeMap

TreeMap implements the Map interface and stores the objects in the pair of key and value. TreeMap class extends AbstractMap class and implements NavigableMap interface to achieve the features of Map and Red-Black tree data structure. TreeMap is sorted and sorts the objects based on supplied comparator at the time of declaration, or if there is no comparator specified, then it sorts the objects according to natural order of its key.

TreeMap is not synchronized and thread safe, we need to explicitly make the TreeMap thread safe, so that only one thread can perform read and write operation at a time. We can make a TreeMap thread safe by using the synchronized() method of Collections interface.

```
Collections.synchronizedSortedMap(new TreeMap(<NameOfTreeMap>));
```

A TreeMap implementation provides guaranteed time cost *log(n)* for the operations like get, put and remove. TreeMap is fail-fast which means iterators returned by iterator method will get modified by others than its own remove() method and will generate **ConcurrentModificationException**. Hence, we cannot put any object after the creation of iterator, but we can remove the object only.

Conclusion

Collection is a power framework which makes the job of a developer easy to manage the list of long elements or objects. This is part of **java.util** package and all Collection interfaces and classes are part of util package.

Collection classes use methods of collection interface to perform operations like add, remove, modify, retrieve, contains, and many more.

In the next chapter, we will discuss the file systems in Java and the different types of classes present in Java programming to read, write, and manage various kinds of files like text file, image file, PDF, word document, and many others.

Points to remember

- List, Queue, Set, and Map are the four major implementations of Collections framework.
- ArrayList and Vector are dynamic arrays. They increase their size dynamically and auto increase and decrease the size of the list as the elements get added or removed. ArrayList increases its size by half of the current array size and vector increases the size to double of the current vector size.
- HashSet internally uses HashMap to store the object. HashSet objects are stored as keys and as their value a constant Object PRESENT is mapped.
- Queue is a data structure that manages the data and implements FIFO (First In First Out) policy with elements. But some queue is not bound with FIFO order, like LinkedList that can be ordered based on the supplied comparator.

Multiple choice questions

1. **Is vector synchronized?**
    a. Yes
    b. No

2. **Which among the following is True?**
   a. ArrayList is synchronized and Vector is not.
   b. ArrayList automatically increases its size by half of the current array size.
   c. Vector automatically increases its size by half of the size of current vector size.
   d. Lists do not accept null elements.

3. **Which among following is not a collection interface?**
   a. List
   b. Array
   c. Set
   d. Queue

4. **Which method is used to remove an element from queue that does not throw an exception?**
   a. delete()
   b. remove()
   c. poll()
   d. truncate()

5. **Using which method we add an object into Map?**
   a. add()
   b. put()
   c. offer()
   d. push()

6. **HashMap may store duplicate keys. Is this statement true or false?**
   a. True
   b. False

Answers

1. a
2. b
3. b

4. c
5. b
6. b

Questions

1. Write a program using HashMap and put numbers 1 to 10 using iterator?
2. What is the difference between ArrayList and LinkedList?
3. What is the difference between ArrayList and Vector?
4. What are some major differences between HashMap and HashSet?
5. What is the difference between the PriorityQueue and Dqueue?
6. Write a program using LinkedHashMap and perform add and remove operation.

Key terms

- **Synchronized**: Program executing two or more threads at the same time.
- **Concurrent**: Operating two or more tasks at the same time in parallel.
- **Iterate**: Read the elements one by one element from a list collection.
- **Mapping**: Pairing key with their value.

Glossary

- https://docs.oracle.com/en/java/javase/11/docs/api/java.base/java/util/Queue.html
- https://docs.oracle.com/javase/8/docs/api/java/util/Collection.html

CHAPTER 13
File Input/Output

In this chapter, we will discuss creating and performing operations on files using Java programming. Java has File API from the beginning of the Java 1.0, which provides various methods for a developer to work and perform operations with files. Java package java.io contains all the classes and interfaces that are required to implement the file input or output.

Other than this, we will also do some deep dive into serialization and deserialization of objects to streams of bytes and bytes to objects.

Structure

In this chapter, we will cover the advanced feature of Java programming, the collection framework:

- The File system
- Input stream
- Output stream
- Buffer
- Writer

- Reader
- Serialization / Deserialization

Objectives

This chapter is to make the student conversant with file and input output terms with respect to Java programming. After going through this chapter, a student can explain the File, the input and output objects, and use these concepts in their programming life. After successful completion of this chapter, you will be able to explain the various terms used in file or input and output streams. You will also be able to write and understand Java programs and applications using the file and perform operations on the file stored in the file system. We will also discuss the serialization and deserialization and how these help in transmission and communication with different applications and software, mainly in terms of API and web services.

Other than that, we will see some of the reader and writer class with use cases with the help of sample programs.

Input and output are important programming concepts to deal with different types of files and perform read, write, and delete operations with the file from or in the file system. Java.io is the package of classes since Java 1.0 to handle files. In Java 7, we have got one more package **`java.nio.file`** that has advanced levels of methods designed on top of IO and overcome various limitations of the **`java.io.File`**.

Let's understand the different classes of File.

File

The **`File`** class is the class that provides access to the file system to Java Virtual Machine. Using this, we can create and locate the file in the memory of computer. Object of the **`File`** class is immutable, which means once the object has been created, it will never change.

Syntax to declare an object of the **`File`** class is as follows:

```
File newFile = new File(<path including name of the file>);
```

A pathname could be either relative or absolute path. A relative path must be interpreted in terms of information taken from some other pathname or current path of the application, which is typically the path where JVM is running the application and program. An absolute pathname is complete, including drive and directory in which no other information is required to locate the file. By default, the classes in the **`java.io`** package always resolve relative pathnames against the current user directory.

Example: 13.1 Sample program to create a file using File class in Java

```
import java.io.File;
import java.io.IOException;

public class FileExample {

  public static void main(String[] args) throws IOException {
    File newFile = new File("ListOfCities.txt");
    if (newFile.createNewFile()) {
            System.out.println("File created.");
        } else {
            System.out.println("File exists.");
        }
  }
}
```

Output:

```
Problems  Javadoc  Declaration  Console
<terminated> FileExample [Java Application] C:\Program Files\Java\jdk1.8.0_131\bin\javaw.exe (Mar 27, 2021, 9:33:09 AM)
File exists.
```

***Figure 13.1**: Output of the File sample program*

The preceding program will create the file, **`ListOfCities.txt`** under the current project directory, because we have given only the filename as a parameter of the **`File`** class, which will be treated as a relative path by JVM. The next line of code is checking the file presence of file with the same name in the system using the method **`createNewFile()`** that returns true or false. Based on the return of **`createdNewFile`**, we are printing a text message on console; so, in our case, the method returns false. Hence the cursor goes to the else section and prints the message **"`File Exists`"**.

We may also specify the absolute path as an argument of File object that will create the file at the same path.

For example, **`File newFile = new File("D:\sample book\io\ListOfCities.txt");`**

Stream

Stream is the sequence of data flowing from source to destination. Here, source is called input and destination is called output. Input and Output streams support many data types such as character, string, and object.

There are two types of streams - input and output and both implement byte and character type of streams to read and write the data:

- **Byte Streams**: Byte Streams are used to perform input and output of 8-bit bytes. Classes such as **`FileInputStream`** and **`FileOutputStream`** support byte streams.
- **Character Streams**: Character Streams are used to perform input and output of 16-bit Unicode characters. Classes such as **`FileReader`** and **`FileWriter`** support character streams.

Input stream

Input is the process to read the data from any source such as file, device, socket, and console. When a third-party application of human interact with system, the system will expect some input to process further steps. Input Stream helps us to read the bytes coming from external sources. **`InputStream`** is an abstract class and super class of all the input classes. Let's study few input and reader classes in detail.

FileReader

`FileReader` is the class that helps to read the characters or text from file using the default buffer size. This only reads the stream of characters from file and makes a connection with the file.

Syntax to declare an object of the **`FileReader`** class:

```
FileReader fileReaderObj = new FileReader("<File Name>");
```

Consider and use **`FileInputStream`** if we must read the byte of stream, since **`FileReader`** works only for reading the text and characters from file.

FileInputStream

`FileInputStream` is a class that helps us to obtain input byte from file and build a connection between file stored in the storage system and application.

The syntax of **`FileInputStream`** constructor for opening connection to a file, the parameter object or name is the file stored in the file system:

```
FileInputStream(File fileObject) or FileInputStream(String fileName)
```

This class has the following methods that are considered important and few of the methods are mandatory to be implemented by classes that use **`FileInputStream`**:

- **`read()`**: This method returns an integer value and reads a byte of data from the input stream. The Read method may or may not have an argument of length of bytes.
- **`close()`**: This method is of the type void and doesn't return any value. This is used to close the input stream and releases system resources associated with the stream.
- **`finalize()`**: This method is of type void and doesn't return anything. Finalize method ensures that the close() method has been executed on the input stream after reading all the inputs and releases all the references so that this can clear the memory.
- **`available()`**: This method returns an integer value that provides estimate of the number of remaining bytes that can be read from the input.
- **`skip()`**: This method returns a long value and takes a long value as an argument and skips over and discards specified number of bytes of data from the input stream.

From the preceding list of methods, read and close must be implemented by all classes. Other than those are optional method and their implementation depends upon the scenario and developer.

Output stream

Output stream writes data as an output into an array or file or any output device. This is an abstract class, and its sub-classes get implemented to generate the output. Classes that are part of output streams are **`BufferedOutputStream`**, **`ByteArrayOutputStream`**, FileOutputStream, and **`ObjectOutputStream`**. Let's discuss few of the output streams in detail.

FileOutputStream

FileOutputStream is used to create a file in the filesystem and write data into that file. If you try to write data into an existing file using *FileOutputStream* and that named file doesn't exist in the file system, then *FileOutputStream* will create a file with given name and add the data into it.

Let's see the syntax for creating **`FileOutputStream`**:

```
OutputStream f = new FileOutputStream("path of the file. Or object of the
File class")
```

To create a file using *FileOutputStream,* we need to pass an argument that will call the constructor and create the file. The argument can be an absolute or relative path of the file, or an object of File class, as given in the preceding syntax.

Example 13.2: Program to read the text from a file using **`BufferedReader`** with **`FileReader`**:

```
import java.io.FileOutputStream;
import java.io.IOException;
import java.io.OutputStream;


public class OutputStreamExample {


  public static void main(String args[]) {
    try {
      OutputStream oStream = new FileOutputStream("Output.txt");
      oStream.write(70);
      oStream.write(65);
      oStream.write(78);
      oStream.close();
      System.out.println("Successfully created and written the file.");
    } catch (IOException e) {
      System.out.print("Exception");
    }
  }
}
```

Output:

```
Problems  Javadoc  Declaration  Console
<terminated> OutputStreamExample [Java Application] C:\Program Files\Java\jdk1.8.0_131\bin\javaw.exe (
Successfully created and written the file.
```

***Figure 13.2**: Output of above file program OutputStreamExample*

The preceding program will successfully create a file **`Output.txt`** in the current directory and write the Unicode characters for numbers 70, 65, and 78 (FAN). The following figure shows the content of the **`Output.txt`** file:

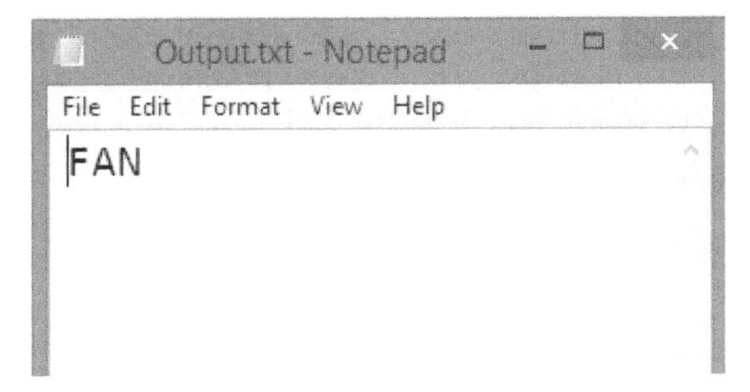

Figure 13.3: Output.txt file content

To write the string into the file, we must convert the byte of String into the byte array and then use the write method to write the byte of array to file. For example:

```
String s="FileOutputStream Java IO example.";
byte b[] = s.getBytes(); //This line is converting string s into byte
array b.
oStream.write(b); // writing byte b into the file.
```

NOTE: The FileOutputStream is mainly used for writing streams of raw bytes such as data of image or video file. For writing the streams of characters into a file, we should consider using the FileWriter class.

Writer

Writer class is an abstract class that helps to write the streams of characters. There is no direct implementation of the `Writer` class, but we use its sub-classes to perform the write operation on file. The methods `write()`, `close()`, and `flush()`, must be implemented by sub-classes of the `Writer` class:

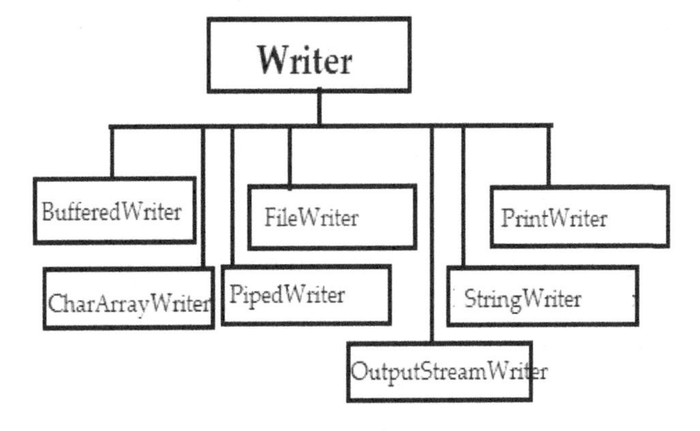

Figure 13.4: Classes and sub classes within the Writer class

Some of the well-known sub-classes of the **Writer** class are **BufferedWriter**, **CharArrayWriter**, **FilterWriter**, **OutputStreamWriter**, **PipedWriter**, **PrintWriter**, and **StringWriter**. We will discuss few classes in detail in this chapter with examples.

FileWriter

The **FileWriter** class is used to write the text to character files using a default buffer size. **FileWriter** writes streams of characters and encodes the characters into bytes using charset. This class is inherited from the class **OutputStreamWriter**. All features and methods of the **OutputStreamWriter** class can be used with **FileWriter** also.

Here is the syntax to declare an object of the **FileWriter** class:

```
FileWriter fileWriterObj = new FileWriter (File file);
```

The preceding statement of code will create an object of **FileWriter** and open the specified file to write the characters with default charset. If we want to specify the **charset** also, then we can add one more parameter in this default constructor:

```
FileWriter fileWriterObj = new FileWriter (File file, Charset charset);
```

FileWriter does not work to store the stream of raw bytes. If we need to store stream of the bytes into a file, we should use **FileOutputStream**.

All File and IO classes implement **AutoCloseable** and **Flushable** interfaces. **AutoCloseable** helps us automatically trigger the **close()** method of the object of that class when the program exits from try-with-resources block. To understand the try-with-resources, please revisit try with resources section in *Chapter 11 Exception and Error Handling*. In try-with-resources, we declare the object of classes before opening the try block in the resource specification header. Resource header specification may contain the declaration of more than one object separated by comma. Here is the example statement:

```
try ( FileWriter fw=new FileWriter(),
InputStreamReader isr = new InputStreamReader() ) {
  //statements
}
```

The preceding snippet of code is a sample to write the code with try-with-resources and declare one or more objects in the resource specification header.

StringWriter

The String Writer class is a writer class that extends the Writer and part of **java.io** package. **StringWriter** writes the characters into a String buffer and then creates a string from it. The **write()** method of string writer class writes the data into the string writer. Hence its required to call the **`write()`** method to add some data into string writer. Other than the writer() method, it has few more methods such as **`append()`**, **`getBuffer()`**, **`close()`**, **`flush()`**, and **`toString()`**.

Here is the syntax of creating an object of the string writer class and writing some data into it:

```
StringWriter stringWriter = new StringWriter();


stringWriter.write("String Writer Data");
```

In the preceding code statements, we have created the object **`stringWriter`** of the class **`StringWriter`** in line one. And in the second line of code, we are writing a string value into it with the help of write method. Now, let's see how we can get this data into a string buffer:

```
StringBuffer stringBuffer = stringWriter.getBuffer();
```

Here, the code statement will put the data from string writer object to a string buffer object. The method **`getBuffer()`** of the String Writer class makes the data available from buffer to string.

Reader

Reader is an abstract class that helps us to read the stream of bytes or characters from console or file. The reader class cannot be implemented directly, but it can be implemented using its sub-classes. Here is the hierarchy diagram of the reader class and its sub-classes:

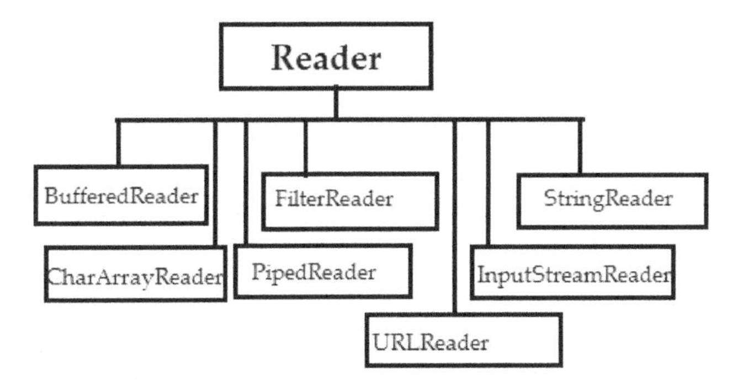

Figure 13.5: Reader class hierarchy and its sub-classes

In the Reader class, **BufferedReader**, **CharArrayReader**, **FilterReader**, **InputStreamReader**, **PipedReader**, **StringReader**, and **URLReader** are the sub-classes. All these classes should implement the **`read()`** method of the reader class to read the bytes and the **`close()`** method after completion of read operation.

Let's discuss few of the sub-classes in detail.

InputStreamReader

The InputStreamReader, a sub-class of the Reader class is a bridge from byte streams to character streams. This reads bytes and decodes those bytes into characters using specific charsets.

For example:

`InputStreamReader (InputStream in)` is the declaration of **`InputStreamReader`** with default charset.

`InputStreamReader (InputStream in, String charset)` is the declaration of **`InputStreamReader`** with given String type charset.

Example 13.2: Example of **`InputStreamReader`** class program:

```
import java.io.BufferedReader;
import java.io.FileInputStream;
import java.io.IOException;
import java.io.InputStreamReader;

public class BufferReaderExample {

  public static void main(String[] args) {
    try {
      FileInputStream file = new FileInputStream("ListOfCities.txt");
      BufferedReader reader = new BufferedReader(new
InputStreamReader(file));
      String line;
      while((line = reader.readLine()) != null){
        System.out.println(line);
      }
    } catch (IOException e) {
      e.printStackTrace();
    }
  }
}
```

Output:

```
3⊖ import java.io.BufferedReader;
4  import java.io.FileInputStream;
5  import java.io.IOException;
6  import java.io.InputStreamReader;
7
8  public class BufferReaderExample {
9
10⊖     public static void main(String[] args) {
11         try {
12             FileInputStream file = new FileInputStream("ListOfCit
13             BufferedReader reader = new BufferedReader(new InputS
14             String line;
15             while((line = reader.readLine()) != null){
16                 System.out.println(line);
17             }
18         } catch (IOException e) {
19             e.printStackTrace();
20         }
21     }
22 }
```

```
Problems  Javadoc  Declaration  Console
<terminated> BufferReaderExample [Java Application] C:\Program Files\Java\jdk1.8.0_131\bin\javaw.exe (N
NewDelhi
Mumbai city
Navi Mumbai
Kolkata
```

***Figure 13.6**: Output of program example 13.2*

In the preceding program, we used the **`ListOfCities.txt`** file as an input source. The **`FileInputStream`** is used to create a bridge between file and Java application, and locating specified file from the file system.

The file **ListOfCities.txt** contains the names of four cities as shown in the console output. Here is the screenshot of the **ListOfCities** file content:

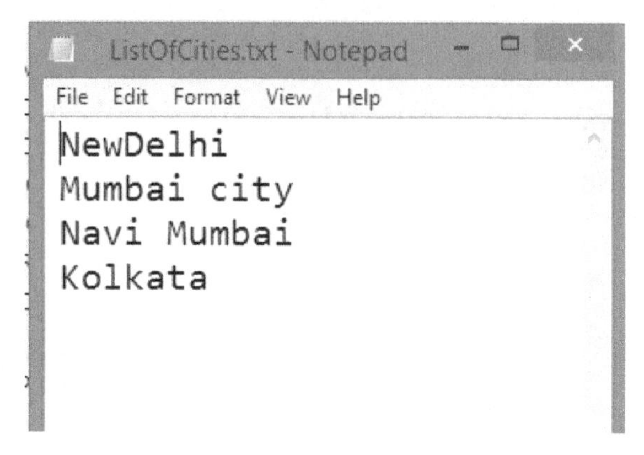

***Figure 13.7**: Snapshot of text file ListOfCities that is being used in Example 13.2*

BufferedReader

The **BufferedReader** class is a subclass of the **Reader** class that reads text or buffering characters or character input stream and provides efficient reading of characters, lines or arrays. We may specify the size of buffer if we want to deal with huge input streams, or just use with the default buffer size. This can be used with **FileReader** or **InputStreamReader** or other readers classes to read the byte of inputs from file or stream and return serialized and deserialized data.

Here is the syntax to declare **BufferedReader** by specifying size:

```
BufferedReader  bReader = new BufferedReader(readerObject)
```

Syntax to declare **BufferedReader** by specifying size:

```
BufferedReader  bReader = new BufferedReader(readerObject, int size)
```

Example 13.3: Program to read the text from a file using **BufferedReader** with **FileReader**:

```
import java.io.BufferedReader;
import java.io.FileReader;
import java.io.IOException;

public class FileAndBufferedReader
{
  public static void main(String[] args) throws IOException
  {
```

```
        FileReader fReader = new FileReader("SampleFile.txt");
        BufferedReader bReader = new BufferedReader(fReader);
        int records;
        while((records = bReader.read()) != -1) {
          System.out.print((char)records);
        }
        bReader.close();
        fReader.close();
    }
}
```

Output:

```
Problems  @ Javadoc  Declaration  Console
<terminated> FileAndBufferedReader [Java Application] C:\Program Files\Java\jdk1.8.0_131\bin\javaw.exe (Mar 28, 2021, 10:57:
Indian cricket team defeated Autrian cricket team in OID match held in New Delhi.
Virat Kohli elected as a new chairman of DDCA.
```

***Figure 13.8**: Output of the Example 13.3*

The preceding Java program shows the implementation of the **FileReader** class to open connection with a file **SampleFile.txt** stored in the file system. Here, the **BufferedReader** class helps to read the characters from a specified file object.

After completion of the read operation, we close the objects and remove the references with the help of the close() method at the end of the program.

NOTE: It is recommended to execute the close method for all Reader and File classes after completion of operation. If we do not close the connections, it might cause memory issue or threshold of number of open connections.

Serialization and Deserialization

Serialization is the process of transforming an object of Java into a stream of bytes. When we serialize an object, it means we are actually converting its state to a stream of bytes, so that the stream of bytes can be later converted into a copy of the Java object. We can make a Java object serializable by implementing the java.io.Serializable interface or its sub interface, **java.io.Externalizable**. Serialization can be implemented to persist the state of any object, and travel or pass that object over the network so that the other system or application can consume or use that stream of bytes. This also helps us to store the state of object into a file or database as permanent storage. Stream of bytes are platform-independent, which means we can serialize and deserialize on any machine or platform, and that can be read and understood by any system. Mainly, we use the approach of serialization when we have some data or file, which we want to transfer to other systems/applications or communicate with external applications.

Serializable is a marker interface, and a marker interface doesn't have any method or member. This marks a Java class so that objects of that class have certain additional capabilities and JVM treats those objects in a different way.

Serializable saves or persists only non-static member of the object; static members of an object will not get serialized. In case we do not want to serialize any non-static member of the class, then we may declare that member transient. If we try to serialize an object that doesn't support serialization, then the system will throw **NotSerializableException** for that.

Deserialization is the opposite of serialization, where we transform a stream of bytes into a Java object.

ObjectOutputStream and **ObjectInputStream** are the IO classes that have the **writeObject** and **readObject** methods, which help us to write and read the state of an object for its class. The **writeObject()** method is responsible for writing the state of the object for its class and **readObject()** method is responsible for reading from the stream and restoring the fields of classes.

Serial version UID:

The class which implements serialization will get a long unique version UID. This UID is automatically generated by the compiler or we may explicitly assign a unique long value to it. Serial version UID is very useful in terms of mapping and identifying the right class, that helps JVM check whether the sender and receiver of a serialized object are loading to the same class or not. If the UID doesn't match, the compiler will throw **InvalidClassException**.

For example:

```
private static final long serialversionUID = 123456789001L;
```

The preceding statement is an example of **serialversionUID** generated for a serializable class.

Conclusion

File input and output are the ways to perform operations with file using Java programming. Input stream is to read the bytes or characters from file and output stream is to write bytes and characters into a file in the file system. We use **FileReader** and **FileWriter** classes to read and write the streams of characters, respectively, and **FileInputStream** and **FileOutputStream** classes to read and write the streams of raw bytes, respectively.

We can use try-with-resources to get rid of explicitly writing the **`close()`** method for that object. The classes that implement **`AutoCloseable`** interface can be declared in the resource specification header and after the execution of the try block, JVM automatically triggers the close method for that object and frees all the references.

In the next chapter, we will discuss the Threads in Java and the different approaches to create the thread and develop and design multi-thread application programming. A thread makes our program faster and prioritizes the execution of thread so that the application can execute in a proper way. We will learn all these things related to Thread and the methods available in Java programming language to perform the operation with threads.

Points to remember

- Every FileReader class throws FileNotFound exception when the specified file or path doesn't exist in the file system.
- System will throw FileNotFoundException when we try to read a File, which is not present in the directory.
- System.in is the input stream to read the user inputs from console. Similarly, System.out is for output stream and System.err is to display the error.

Multiple choice questions

1. **Which among following is not a sub-class of Reader class?**
   a. FileReader
   b. BufferedReader
   c. InputStreamReader
   d. File
2. **Which exception will a program generate when a specified file name doesn't exist in the file system?**
   a. OutOfBoundException
   b. FileNotFoundException
   c. NullPointerException
   d. NoException
3. **Which of the following classes is used to write the image data?**
   a. FileOutputStream
   b. FileWriter

c. OutputStream
d. StreamWriter

4. **FileWriter class extends which writer class?**
   a. OutputStreamWriter
   b. Writer
   c. File
   d. AutoCloseable

5. **Which interface is used to make a class serializable?**
   a. Serial
   b. StreamableValue
   c. Externalize
   d. Serializable

Answers

1. **d**
2. **b**
3. **a**
4. **a**
5. **d**

Questions

1. Write a program using FileReader to read a text from a file stored on the local system. File name should be "Fruits.txt" and contain at least names of 10 fruits.
2. What is the difference between Byte stream and Character Stream?
3. What is charset and what all types of charsets are present? Write a note.
4. What is deserialization?

Key terms

- **Stream**: Stream is the sequence of data flowing from source to destination.
- **Byte:** Byte is the unit to measure of size of information or data on computer.

- **Charset**: It is a named mapping between sequences of sixteen-bit Unicode(UTF-16) characters and bytes.
- **File system**: File system manages how and where data on a storage disk, usually a hard disk drive (HDD) is stored.
- **File**: File is the permanent storage that stores some content. For example, text file, PDF, word file, image file, and so on.
- **Serialization**: Serialization is the process of converting a java object into stream of bytes or characters.
- **Deserialization:** Deserialization is the process to converting stream of bytes or characters into a Java object.

Glossary

- Javadoc FileInputStream https://docs.oracle.com/javase/7/docs/api/java/io/FileInputStream.html
- https://docs.oracle.com/en/java/javase/11/docs/api/java.base/java/io/Reader.html
- https://docs.oracle.com/en/java/javase/11/docs/api/java.base/java/nio/charset/Charset.html
- https://docs.oracle.com/javase/tutorial/essential/io/file.html
- https://docs.oracle.com/en/java/javase/11/docs/api/java.base/java/io/FileWriter.html
- https://docs.oracle.com/en/java/javase/11/docs/api/java.base/java/io/FileOutputStream.html
- https://docs.oracle.com/en/java/javase/11/docs/api/java.base/java/lang/AutoCloseable.html
- https://docs.oracle.com/javase/7/docs/api/java/io/Serializable.html

CHAPTER 14
Thread

In this chapter, we will discuss the Thread and process. Thread is the smallest unit of execution of program, where we utilize the CPU idle state and give chance to other threads to execute, which is called multithreading. Multithreading is the conceptual programming model in which one program is divided into subprograms that can concurrently execute. We will discuss the concept of multithreading in detail in this chapter. We will also discuss the thread and process in detail and what all methods are available to handle the multithreading in the Thread class. Also, we will explain the thread priority and how to set and get the priority of thread and different states of thread.

There are various methods that help to handle the multithreaded application like join, wait, sleep, notify, and many more to split the execution process and communicate with threads within the process. We will study all the concepts of thread and multithread in this chapter.

Structure

In this chapter, we will discuss the following topics:

- Thread
- Process and thread

- Multitasking
- Multi-threading
- Creation of Thread
- Lifecycle of thread
- Methods of Thread
- Thread Priority

Objectives

After successful completion of this chapter, you will be able to understand and explain the concept of thread, multitasking, and multithreading. In Java programming, we achieve the concept of the multithreading by extending the Thread class or by implementing the Runnable interface. We will see both the approaches with sample programs in this chapter.

Thread

Thread is the smallest execution unit of a process and a process may have many threads that are executing at the same time. Thread has its own execution path within the process and shares the memory of the process with other threads, which are running in the same process. Thread doesn't allocate any memory, but it uses the memory allocated by its process; this helps faster and efficient communication between threads within the same process.

Process and Thread

In parallel programming, there are two ways to achieve the concurrent execution of a same program or multiple tasks at the same time from an application or program: processor and thread. There is a huge difference between the processor and thread.

Process

A process always allocates separate memory in the system for the execution and has a self-contained execution environment and executes with the same allocated memory. The Java virtual machine runs as a single process and executes java program within the same process, but if needed, we can create additional processes using **`start()`** of the **`ProcessBuilder`** object.

For example:

```
Process p = new ProcessBuilder("customProcess", "args").start();
```

In the following figure, there are three processes executing in the operating system:

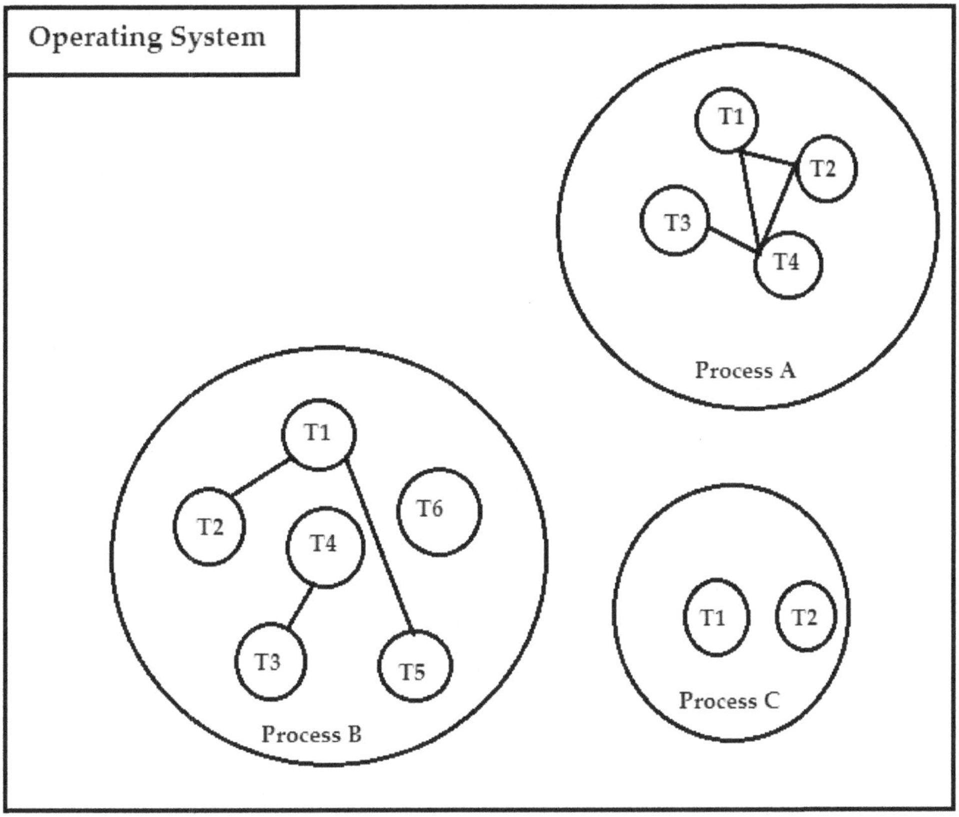

***Figure 14.1**: Threads and processes in the CPU*

Each process has multiple threads executing. In process **A**, six threads are executing, the process **B** has four threads and process **C** has two threads.

> **NOTE: ProcessBuilder is a part of the java.lang package. Each ProcessBuilder instance manages a collection of process attributes.**

Thread

A thread never allocates its own memory; it always uses the memory allocated by the processor and executes within a process. Threads are very lightweight and consume fewer resources for execution. A simple Java program always starts with a main thread, and a thread can also create further threads to lessen the execution of the program:

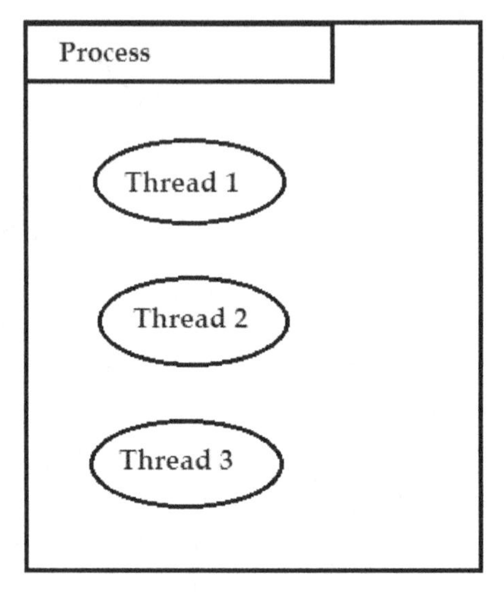

***Figure 14.2**: Multiple Threads are executing in a process*

A thread can communicate with other threads running in the same process using the thread methods such as wait(), notify(), and yield().

Multitasking

Multitasking is the term use to refer when a machine or person is doing or running multiple works or tasks at the same time. For example, when we work on a computer, at the same time, there are multiple programs and applications running such as playing music, writing on a word document, browsing Internet, and many others. So, we can say that our computer is multitasking. On the other hand, if we look at a television and analyze the functionality of a television, we can see that a TV is not a multitasking device because we can't do many things on TV at the same time.

There are two ways to perform and implement multitasking – process based and thread based. Both process and thread enhance the capacity and capability of a system for concurrent execution.

The following figure shows the different tasks that are being performed at the same time using a single computer:

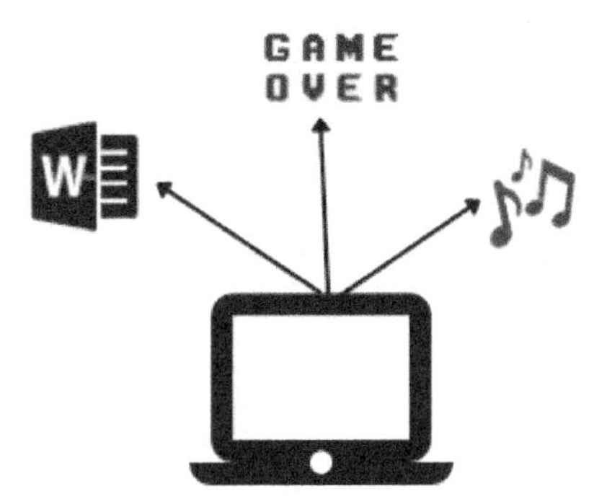

Figure 14.3: *An example of multitasking in computer*

A person may play music, write on a word document, and play a game at the same time on a computer.

There is no multitasking where multiple tasks are being executed on the CPU. But it is all about utilizing the CPU's ideal time and allowing other processes or threads to execute, when one program is waiting for input or other resources.

Multithreading

Multithreading is the concept to executing multiple threads concurrently. A thread is lightweight and sequential control of flow within a process. A single-threaded process follows a single sequence of control during execution. A multithreaded process has numerous sequences of control; therefore, the multithreaded process is capable of performing several independent actions at the same time. This is all about allowing the other threads to execute from the same process. A multithreaded application speeds up the processes and execution of a program, boosts the efficiency of objects, and completes the task in less time by utilizing the CPU, which is not possible in a single thread application.

This way we improve the responsiveness of an application and ensure the program is running even when other threads are waiting for any external resource or input from the user.

The following figure shows how a Java program is divided into sub programs that can run at the same time in parallel to each other:

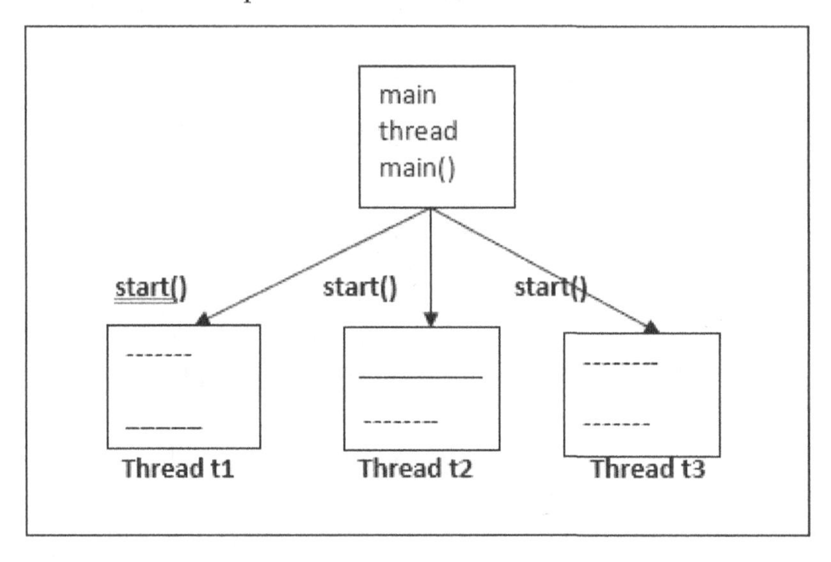

***Figure 14.4**: A single application split into multithreaded application in Java*

Here, the main thread of Java program, the **main()** method is a **NORM_PRIORITY** thread and entry point of a program. Then further in the main, we have created three threads **t1**, **t2**, and **t3** that run in parallel to each other and execute the program in multiple flows.

In Java programming, there are two ways to implement multithreading and develop a multithreaded application, either by implementing the **java.lang.Runnable** interface or by inheriting the **java.lang.Thread** class. We will discuss both the ways in detail with example in this chapter.

Creation of thread

In Java programming, there are two ways to create a thread class, the first is by inheriting the Thread class and second is by implementing the Runnable thread.

Using the Thread class

The first approach to create a thread is by inheriting the Thread class to our class. **Java.lang.Thread** is the **Thread** class, which can be inherited by sub classes to declare and use a thread. A class inherits the Thread class with the help of the extends keyword. Here is the declaration of a Thread class:

```
public class MyThreadClass extends Thread {
  public void run() {
```

```
// do something here
}
}
```

A class that extends the thread class must have to override the **run()** method of the thread class, that is, the entry point of a thread execution.

Example 14.1: A sample program to create a Thread using **Thread** class:

```
class MyThreadClass extends Thread {
   public void run() {
      System.out.println("Hello");
   }
}
public class MainClass {
   public static void main(String s[]) {
      MyThreadClass t1=new MyThreadClass ();
      MyThreadClass t2=new MyThreadClass ();
      t1.start();
      t2.start();
   }
}
```

When we execute **t1.start()** (here we are calling thread), it will request call thread to call **run()** method. Every time, the output will depend upon CPU scheduling. But if only **t1.run()** (here we calling a method) is implementing, then we are only calling the method. Here, **t1** and **t2** are two thread objects of the same thread class **MyThreadClass**.

Athreadcannotbestartedtwice.Ifwetrytodoso,**IllegalThreadStateException**will be thrown. The following code snippet will throw **IllegalThreadStateException**:

```
MyThread t1 = new MyThread();
t1.start();
t1.start();
```

The second **start()** method execution on the same thread will throw the exception.

Using the Runnable interface

Another way to create Thread is using the Runnable interface. A class should implement the Runnable interface and override its **run()** method. The run method is the entry point of a thread and starts execution from there when the **start()**

method executed on that thread. Here is the syntax for creating Thread using Runnable interface:

```
public class MyThreadClass implements Runnable {
  public void run () {
    // write your statement here
}
}
```

Let's understand the thread creation using runnable interface with an example.

Example 14.2: A sample program to create a thread using the Runnable interface:

```
public class MainClass {
  public static void main(String[] args) {
    MyThreadClass myThreadClass = new MyThreadClass();
    Thread t1 = new Thread(myThreadClass);
    t1.start();
  }
}

class MyThreadClass implements Runnable{
  @Override
  public void run() {
    System.out.println("Hello");

  }
}
```

Output:

```
Problems  @ Javadoc  Declaration  Console ⊠
<terminated> MainClass [Java Application] C:\Program Files\Java\jre7\bin\javaw.e
Hello
```

Figure 14.5: Output window of the preceding thread program (example 14.2)

When we implement the runnable interface, we must create object of **Thread** class and pass the object of our thread class as a parameter of the **Thread** class. As written in the preceding program, **MyThreadClass** is our **Thread** class, which is implementing the runnable interface. And to start the **Thread** class, we will call the start method on object of the **`Thread`** class, and not on the actual **`Thread`** class, which we created.

Lifecycle of thread

During the execution of threads, a thread keeps changing its state automatically or explicitly by calling the thread methods. From creation of a thread till the end of a thread is called the life cycle of a thread. There are five states of a thread at the high level. The following figure shows all stages of threads during its execution:

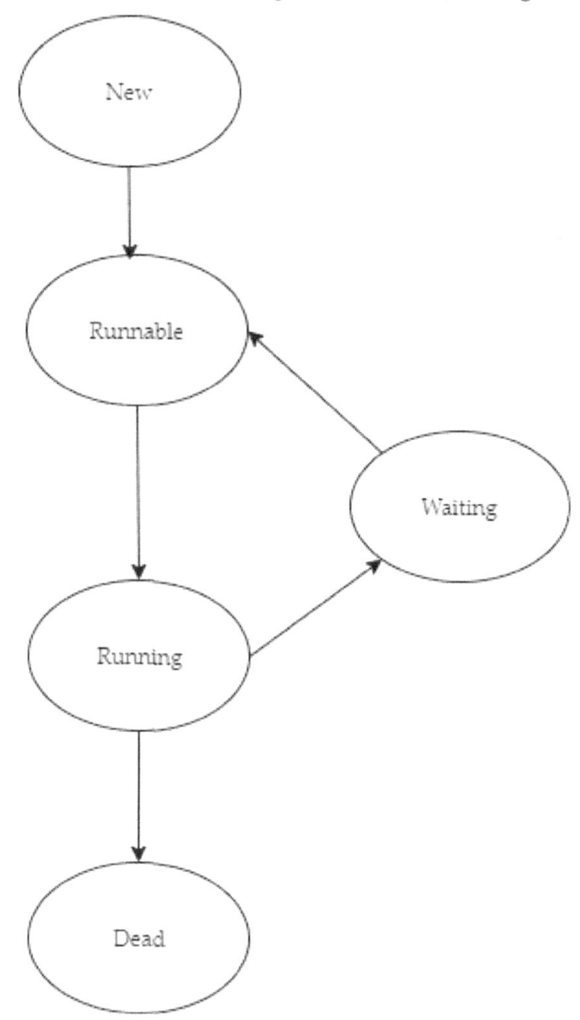

***Figure 14.6**: Different stages of a thread*

- **NEW:** A thread will be in new state once it's declared and remains in that state until we call the start method on that thread object. A newly created thread does not start running automatically, it will always wait for the start method to be called to change the state from new to runnable. No system resources are allocated to this thread and this may also be called empty thread.

- **RUNNABLE:** A thread is moved to runnable state after calling the `start()` method of thread. It is a state when a thread is ready for execution and waiting for the availability of the processor.
- **WAITING:** A thread is in the waiting state to fulfil the dependencies or other prerequisites. A thread moves in this state after executing the wait or join methods, and when `notify()` or `notifyAll()` or `interrupted()` methods get called on the thread object, the thread resumes the execution.
- **RUNNING:** When the run method of a thread is called, the thread moves to running state and starts executing within the process.
- **TERMINATED:** A thread is in the terminated state when it has completed the execution or explicitly stopped by the stop method.

The preceding five states of a thread are the high level of stages. Other than these, the thread also goes into sub-states of the states with the help of different thread methods. Let's take a deep dive into thread methods and see how the thread moves from one stage to another:

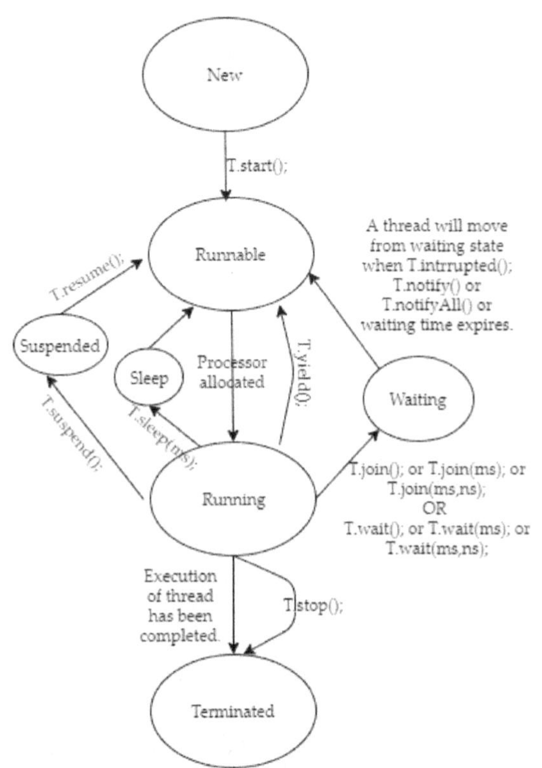

Figure 14.7: *How a thread moves in different states throughout the life cycle*

The **Thread.getState()** method of Thread is used to identify and get the current state of thread. The **getState()** method will return the states of thread among six thread states; they are **new**, **runnable**, **blocked**, **waiting**, **timed_waiting**, and **terminated**. Here, **blocked** and **timed_waiting** are two sub-states of waiting states.

- **BLOCKED**: A thread is in the blocked state because the process or statement of code that is needed to be executed is locked by other thread.
- **TIMED_WAITING**: A thread is in this state with a specified time. A thread will go into this state when the **wait(millisecond)** or **sleep(millisecond)** methods get called on the thread.

The preceding states are known as life cycle of a thread, which are the stages a thread must go through before termination. Thread methods are responsible to move or transmit a thread from one state to another. Here are the methods that we use with threads.

Thread Methods

Thread methods are the methods of the **java.lang.Thread** class, which helps us to manage and deal with the threads. Here are the few methods that are frequently used in Java programming by developers:

- **start()**: A newly created thread does not start running automatically. You need to call the start function. Calling the **start()** method places the virtual CPU alive in the thread into a runnable state.
- **yield()**: This method gives chance to other runnable threads to execute. Yield places the calling thread into a runnable group and allows another runnable thread to run. If no other threads are runnable, yield does nothing.
- **run()**: The **start()** method is used to create new thread; once the thread is created, it requests to call the **run()** function for execution.
- **wait()**: This method is used to push a thread into an object monitor and stop the execution of the thread until awakened by notify, **notifyAll**, or interrupt methods.
- **wait(time)**: This method is used to push a thread into object monitor and stop the execution of the thread for the specified time. The parameter takes long type value that denotes time in millisecond.
- **sleep(time)**: This method will suspend the execution of thread for the specified time. The parameter takes long type value that denotes time in milliseconds.

- **join()**: This method is used to queue up a thread in execution. Once called on thread, the current thread will wait till calling thread completes its execution.
- **join(time)**: This method is used to queue up a thread in execution. After calling this join (millisecond) method, the current thread will wait for the specified time and doesn't wait for the other threads to die or complete the execution.
- **notify()**: This method is used to wake up a single thread that is waiting on this object's monitor. A thread waits on an object monitor by calling the **wait()** method.
- **notifyAll()**: This method is used to wake up all threads that are waiting on this object's monitor.
- **stop()**: This method is used to stop or terminate a thread.
- **suspend()**: This method is used to suspend a thread from getting executed.
- **resume()**: This method will resume the execution of a thread, which was suspended by the **suspend()** method.

There are other methods too, which are used to get the thread details.

Thread Priority

Every thread has a priority in Java programming; that thread priority helps the JRE to prioritize the execution of thread. A thread with high priority always gets executed first. A new thread has its priority initially set equal to the priority of the creating thread and is a daemon thread if and only if the creating thread is a daemon.

There are 10 logical ranges of thread priority; the logical value is an integer number from 1 to 10 and can be set to any thread object using the **setPriority(int)** method. There are three static variables defined in the **Thread** class for priority. Default priority of a Java thread is **NORM_PRIORITY**:

- **MAX_PRIORITY**: The maximum priority that a thread can have. The logical thread value is 10.
- **MIN_PRIORITY**: The minimum priority that a thread can have. The logical thread value is between 1 to 4.
- **NORM_PRIORITY**: The default priority that is assigned to a thread. The logical thread value is between 5 to 9.

To identify and get the priority of an executing thread, we may check with the help of the **getPriority()** method of Thread.

NOTE: If two threads are set with same priority, then we cannot decide and expect which thread will execute first. It depends on the thread scheduler's algorithm (For example Round-Robin, First Come First Serve).

Thread Synchronization

Synchronization is a keyword in the Java programming language that facilitates the programmer to control threads that are sharing data. This is the best approach in Java technology to provide a mechanism to treat the data carefully. Synchronized keywords are used to declare a method or create a method or block of statement thread safe, that means only one thread can access that block of code at a time and other threads will be in a waiting state until the first thread completes the execution. This is done when we want to get the updated data after evaluation or while modifying the object so that other threads get only the updated value after the successful modification of the object. If we do not lock the code block, then other threads may perform the operation on the same object, which causes ambiguity and corrupts the actual data.

Let's illustrate the concept of Thread Synchronization with the help of a program.

Example 14.3: A sample program to show the use of synchronized keyword to implement thread safety:

```
package coreJava;
class SynchronizedEx {
  synchronized void show(String p){
    try {
      System.out.println("*****");
      System.out.print(p);
      Thread.sleep(1000);
      System.out.println("#####");
    }
    catch(InterruptedException e){
      e.printStackTrace();
    }
  }
}
class MyThread implements Runnable {
  Thread c;
  String m;
  SynchronizedEx r;
```

```
  MyThread(SynchronizedEx w, String k) {
    r=w;
    m=k;
    c=new Thread(this);
  }
  public void run(){
    r.show(m);
  }
}
public class test {
  public static void main(String s[])throws InterruptedException {
    SynchronizedEx d=new SynchronizedEx();
    MyThread t1=new MyThread(d,"Hello");
    MyThread t2=new MyThread(d,"JAVA");
    t1.c.start();
    t2.c.start();
    t1.c.join();
    t2.c.join();
  }
}
```

Output:

```
Problems  @ Javadoc  Declaration  Console
<terminated> test [Java Application] C:\Program Files\Java\jre7\bin\javaw.exe (A
*****
Hello#####
*****
JAVA#####
```

Figure 14.8: Output window of the preceding synchronized class

In the preceding program, we have created two threads **t1** and **t2**. The synchronized keyword is used here for that; if **t1** captures the show method first then **t2** cannot share that resource at the same time but can perform other work. Even after executing the join method, **t2** will be unable to run the **show()** method because **t1** was getting executed at that time.

Conclusion

Thread is the smallest unit of execution in any Java program. The main method of a Java program is also a thread and is also the entry point of execution. Using multithreading we split or divide single execution flow of an application into multi execution flows; therefore, multiple threads get executed concurrently in the CPU. This way we also stop, start, set dependencies and release the execution of a thread. In this generation of computers, every application is multithreaded to offer robust performance and efficiency and for perfect utilization of CPU.

Threads never allocate their own memory; they use the memory allocated to processes and threads always get created within the process. A process can have more than one thread, and all can communicate with each other with the help of thread methods.

In the next chapter, we will discuss the Java Database Connectivity (JDBC) API, which helps us to connect Java application with any external data source such as relational database system or spread sheet. These data sources are the permanent storage, and all input and output of Java applications goes to the connected data source.

Points to remember

- A thread is a lightweight process, the smallest unit of code that is dispatched by the scheduler.
- Multithreading is about executing multiple threads of same program simultaneously into an application. A thread gets divided into chunks and become smaller threads and start executing in CPU simultaneously with other threads.
- Synchronized is the keyword to make a code block or method thread safe.
- A thread cannot be started twice. If we try to do so, **`IllegalThreadStateException`** will be thrown.

Multiple choice questions

1. **Which is the correct statement to create a thread?**
   a. Thread t1 = new Thread();
   b. Runnable run = new Thread();
   c. Thread t2 = new Runnable();
   d. Thread thread;

2. **What are the two approaches to create a thread class?**
    a. Implementing Thread interface
    b. Extending Runnable interface
    c. Extending Threading class
    d. Extending Thread class
    e. Implementing run() method
    f. Implementing Runnable interface

3. **What is the default priority of a Java thread?**
    a. MIN_PRIORITY
    b. MAX_PRIROTY
    c. HIGH_PRIORITY
    d. NORM_PRIORITY

4. **Which method is mandatory to be implemented for a thread class?**
    a. start()
    b. join()
    c. create()
    d. run()

5. **Which is not a valid state of a thread?**
    a. Active
    b. New
    c. Runnable
    d. Waiting

Answers

1. a
2. d and f
3. d
4. d
5. a

Questions

1. What is the difference between yield and sleep methods?
2. How the join(1000) is different from wait(1000)?
3. What is the difference between the sleep and wait methods?
4. What is the difference between a process and thread?
5. Predict the output of the following thread program:

```
public class MainClass {
  public static void main(String[] args) {
    MyThreadClass myThreadClass = new MyThreadClass();
    Thread t1 = new Thread(myThreadClass);
    t1.start();
    t1.start();
  }
}

class MyThreadClass implements Runnable{
  @Override
  public void run() {
  }
}
```

6. What is the difference between wait() and wait(time)?

Key terms

- ProcessBuilder
- Demon Thread

Glossary

- https://docs.oracle.com/javase/7/docs/technotes/guides/vm/thread-priorities.html
- https://docs.oracle.com/javase/7/docs/api/java/lang/Thread.html

CHAPTER 15
JDBC

The **Java Database Connectivity** (**JDBC**) API provides universal data access from the Java programming language to access the data from relational database and files. The **`java.sql`** and **`javax.sql`** are the two API packages that provide the implementation of JDBC in Java programming. These APIs help us to read and write the data from data source into the tabular format, which is ResultSet.

Structure

In this chapter, we will see and cover the connectivity of Java application with backend data providers. As part of this chapter, we will cover the following topics:

- Driver
- Api
- Connection
- ResultSet

Objectives

After successfully completion of this chapter, you will be able to understand and work with JDBC and connect with any relational database (RDBMS) system to grab the data. Also, you will be able to query the database to get the data into the result sets.

JDBC

JDBC stands for Java Database Connectivity, which is an API that helps us to connect Java application with any data source like relational database system, spread sheet or any flat file, to get and set the data. There are two packages (**`java.sql`** and **`javax.sql`**) that are available out of the box in the JDK:

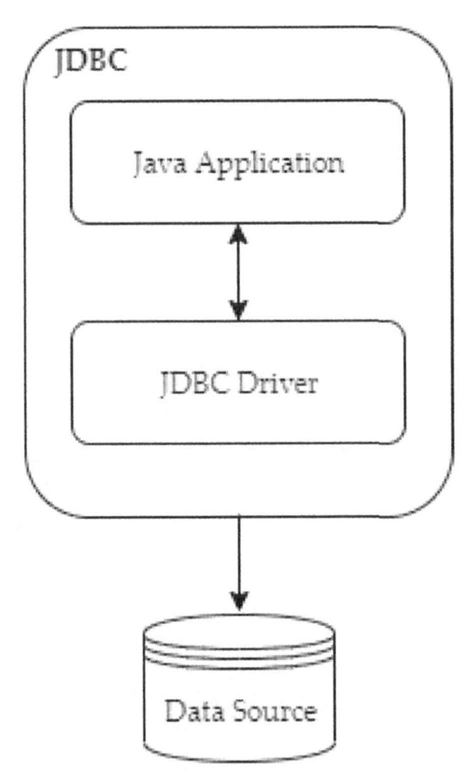

***Figure 15.1**: JDBC components and models*

The preceding diagram shows why a Java application uses JDBC and connects with data source. Let's study different modules and components of JDBC in detail.

Driver

Driver is JDBC a technology-based application that sets up a bridge between source and Java applications. The driver mediates the application and database and retrieves and transmits the data. A JDBC driver might be written using Java programming or in combination of Java programming language and Java native interface method. JDBC drive is different for different database management systems. There are four types of JDBC drivers:

- **JDBC-ODBC driver**: The JDBC-ODBC driver uses the ODBC driver and sets up a bridge to connect with the database.
- **Native-API driver**: This is a partial Java driver that uses client-side libraries of database to connect and communicate with database. This driver must be installed on the client machine.
- **Network Protocol driver**: This is fully written in Java programming. Network protocol uses middleware application server that converts JDBC calls into vendor-specific database protocol.
- **Thin driver**: This is completely written in Java programming language. This converts JDBC calls directly into the vendor-specific database protocol.

There four types of drivers being used by JDBC to connect with different data sources.

Driver Manager

The driver manager API is a fully implemented class, which is responsible to set up a connection with database or data source. The driver manager automatically loads the available JDBC driver to establish the connection with data source.

Query database

JDBC provides few interfaces that help us to execute the SQL statement, stored procedure, and function at database. Here are the few interfaces. All these interfaces will throw SQLException:

- **`Statement`**: Statement is used to execute basic SQL DDL statements to data source:

  ```
  Statement createStatement()
  ```

- **`PreparedStatement`**: Prepared statement is used to send statement or SQL statements to data source. A prepared statement object contains not just an SQL statement, but a precompiled SQL statement. This means that when the prepared statement is executed, the DBMS can just run the prepared statement SQL statement without having to compile it first, which saves the execution time. The prepared statement is used to create a parameterized query:

  ```
  PreparedStatement prepareStatement(String sql)
  ```

This interface takes a String type parameter, which will be the SQL statement.

- **`CallableStatement`**: The callable statement is used to call database stored procedures and function; it extends the prepared statement. The performance of a callable statement is better than the statement and prepared statement:

  ```
  CallableStatement prepareCall(String sql)
  ```

- **`Connection`**: The Connection interface provides methods for creating statements and managing connections and their properties. All SQL statements are executed, and their results returned within the context of a Connection object.

- **`Savepoint`**: Savepoint provides the middle point within a current transaction; that middle point is restored or rolled back to savepoint. When a transaction is rolled back to a savepoint, all changes made after that savepoint are undone. Savepoints can be either named or unnamed:

  ```
  Savepoint setSavepoint()
  ```

  The **`setSavepoint()`** method creates unnamed save point in current transaction; if **`setSavepoint`** is invoked outside of an active transaction, a transaction will be started at this newly created save point.

The following code is a sample java program with implementation of JDBC with MySQL data source:

```
import java.sql.Connection;
import java.sql.DriverManager;
import java.sql.PreparedStatement;
import java.sql.SQLException;

public class JDBCExample {
    private static final String INSERT_SQL = "INSERT INTO employee " +
        "  (empid, name, email, country, password) VALUES " + " (?, ?,
?, ?, ?);";
    private static final String UPDATE_SQL = "update employee set name =
? where id = ?;";

    private static final String jdbcUrl = "jdbc:mysql://localhost:8080/
mysql_database?useSSL=false";
    private static final String username = "admin";
    private static final String password = "admin";

    public static void main(String[] args) {
        try (Connection conn = DriverManager.getConnection(jdbcUrl,
```

```
username, password);) {
            conn.setAutoCommit(false);
            try (PreparedStatement insertStmt = conn.
prepareStatement(INSERT_SQL); PreparedStatement updateStmt = conn.
prepareStatement(UPDATE_SQL);) {
                // Create insert statement with parameterized values
             insertStmt.setInt(1, 200);
                insertStmt.setString(2, "java7");
                insertStmt.setString(3, "java7@mail.com");
                insertStmt.setString(4, "IN");
                insertStmt.setString(5, "password@123");

                // Execute the insert statement to feed the table
                insertStmt.executeUpdate();

                // Commit the changes into database
                conn.commit();


                System.out.println("Data inserted and committed
successfully.");
            } catch (SQLException e) {
             System.out.println(e);
                if (conn != null) {
                    try {
                        // Roll back transaction
                        System.out.println("Transaction is being rolled
back.");
                        conn.rollback();
                    } catch (Exception ex) {
                        ex.printStackTrace();
                    }
                }
            }
        } catch (SQLException e) {
            System.out.println(e);
        }
    }
}
```

Output:

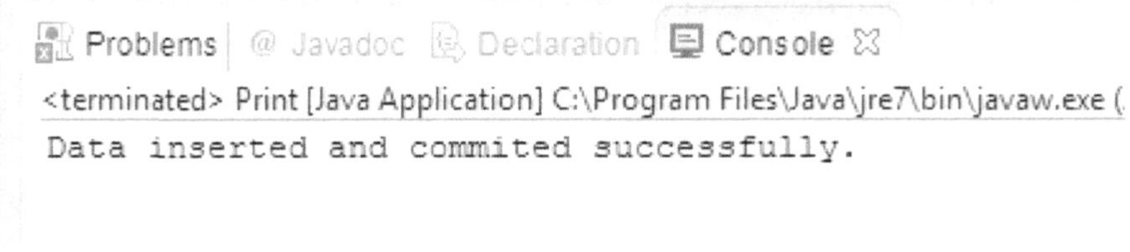

Problems @ Javadoc Declaration Console
<terminated> Print [Java Application] C:\Program Files\Java\jre7\bin\javaw.exe (
Data inserted and commited successfully.

Figure 15.2: Screenshot of output of the preceding JDBC program

ResultSet

The **ResultSet** is an interface that provides methods for retrieving and manipulating the results and is generated on the execution of SQL queries on database. By default, the result set is one directional and non-updatable. We can read data sequentially, starting from the first row to last row, and cannot modify the data into result set. There are three types of result sets as follows:

- **TYPE_FORWARD_ONLY**: The result set cannot be scrolled; its cursor moves forward only, from before the first row to after the last row. The rows contained in the result set depend on how the underlying database generates the results. That is, it contains the rows that satisfy the query at either the time the query is executed or as the rows are retrieved. This is the default result set type.
- **TYPE_SCROLL_INSENSITIVE**: The result can be scrolled; its cursor can move both forward and backward relative to the current position, and it can move to an absolute position. The result set is insensitive to changes made to the underlying data source while it is open. It contains the rows that satisfy the query at either the time the query is executed or as the rows are retrieved.
- **TYPE_SCROLL_SENSITIVE**: The result can be scrolled; its cursor can move both forward and backward relative to the current position, and it can move to an absolute position. The result set reflects changes made to the underlying data source, while the result set remains open.

All databases do not support all types of result sets. To check what all result sets a database supports, we may call the method **DatabaseMetaData.supportsResultSetType(<ResultsetType>);** if this method returns **true** for the specified **ResultSet** type, it is supported; otherwise, return **false**. We can check the same for the concurrency level also with the help of **DatabaseMetaData.supportsResultSetConcurrency(<specifyConcurrency>)**.

RowSet

RowSet objects are derived from the **`ResultSet`** interface and all RowSets have the capabilities of result set. The RowSet has some additional feature properties, JavaBean notification, and scroll ability or updatability; these all are not present in **`ResultSet`**:

- First, properties are the fields of table that has its corresponding setter and getter methods.
- Second, RowSet objects use the JavaBeans event model, in which registered components are notified when certain events occur. The Cursor movement, insert or update or delete row, and change in contents of RowSet are the three types of events that generate notifications.
- Third, RowSet is scrollable and updatable by default, every object of RowSet have the scroll feature to read the rows from result.

RowSet interface extends the standard **`java.sql.ResultSet`** interface. The RowSet interface provides a set of properties that allow RowSet instance to be configured to connect to a JDBC data source and read some data from the data source. There are two types of RowSets:

- **Connected Rowset**: A connected RowSet makes connection with data source and keeps the connection open throughout its life cycle.
- **Disconnected Rowset**: A disconnected RowSet does not keep the connection always open with data source. It opens the connection to get the data and after that, it is disconnected.

RowSet is easy to use and very useful in reading the data from data source.

NOTE: ResultSet is dependent on the driver to support the scrollable feature, but RowSet always supports scroll feature without any dependency. Hence, if we want scroll and update feature on a result set, then convert it into a row set.

Conclusion

Java application communicates and connects with external data sources (like database or spreadsheet or file) to get the data for application. Java database connectivity is an out of the box API that eases the task of developer to connect with various databases. JDBC provides inbuilt drivers and interfaces to query the database for the right data.

JDBC APIs are very powerful features of java programming that helps the developers in their daily life to deal with types of data stored on data sources other than Java.

In the next chapter, we will discuss the management of memory and how JDK handles and manages the memory automatically by executing the different levels of garbage collections that check and reclaim the memory from dead objects. Garbage collection is a powerful feature of JDK that keeps the memory available for new objects and Java programs or applications active and running. We will discuss all these in detail in the next chapter.

Points to remember

- DriverManager is responsible to set up a connection with database or data source.
- ResultSet gets created with the result that returns after execution of SQL statement.

Multiple choice questions

1. **Which of these is not a type of result?**
   a. TYPE_FORWARD_ONLY
   b. HOLD_CURSORS_OVER_COMMIT
   c. TYPE_SCROLL_INSENSITIVE
   d. TYPE_SCROLL_SENSITIVE

2. **Which type of statement is used to call a function of database?**
   a. CallableStatement
   b. PreparedStatement
   c. Statement
   d. FunctionStatement

Answers

1. b
2. a

Questions

1. What are the types of Resultset?
2. What is the role of DriverManager in JDBC?

3. What are the differences between PreparedStatement and CallableStatement?

Key terms

- **SQL**: Structured query language
- **DDL**: Data definition language
- **JDBC**: Java database connectivity
- **Data Source**: Permanent storage of data either in database or file.

Glossary

- https://docs.oracle.com/javase/7/docs/api/java/sql/Connection.html
- https://docs.oracle.com/javase/tutorial/jdbc/basics/retrieving.html

CHAPTER 16
Memory Management

In this chapter, we will discuss the Java memory management and how Java virtual machine (JVM) automatically manages memory for executing the Java application and program. Heap is the memory that gets created within the RAM for random access, where classes, objects and members created. Garbage collection is the backbone of JVM for dealing with memory and allocating and reclaiming the memory from heap.

Heap and sack are the random memory types and heap is major memory, which is being use by Java programming. Heap memory is further classified into the three logical parts called generations - new, old, and permanent are the three generations of the heap memory. All three generations of memory are managed and handled by minor, major, and full garbage collection that helps to reclaim the unused memory from system by deleting the unreferenced objects from heap.

Structure

In this chapter, we will cover and have a detailed discussion on management of memory and how JVM manages the memory for Java programs. As part of this chapter, let us discuss the following topics of memory management:

- Garbage collection and its types
- Finalize

- Heap size
- Dealing with heap memory

Objectives

After successful completion of this chapter, you will be able to understand and explain the garbage collection and garbage collector and its role in managing the memory for Java applications.

Also, you will be able to understand the process of increasing and decreasing the size of heap memory and how to set memory for any generation and application by instructing JVM with –XX parameters.

Garbage collection

Garbage collection (GC) is the process of memory management that finds and removes or cleans the unused heap memory allocated to the objects and keeps the memory reusable and available for new resources. Garbage collection executes automatically and removes the allocated memory for only those objects and members that do not hold any references and no more in use, or in general terms, we can say reclaims the unused heap memory. When we execute a Java program in a machine, it requires the memory.

The heap is a memory where Java objects live at runtime for processes and operations, and this is the only memory that gets managed by garbage collection that also ensures and makes available the required free memory for execution of Java programs. **Java virtual memory** (JVM) provides various garbage collectors that help the system or operating system to improve the performance and efficiency of the memory.

There are two methods `Runtime.gc()` and `System.gc()` that generate and send the request to JVM for garbage collection. We cannot force the garbage collectors to reclaim the unused memory, JVM automatically manages all these to run the application or program and a developer need not worry about the memory management in Java. GC can be forcefully executed with the help of any of the following methods:

- `System.gc();`
- `Runtime.getRuntime().gc();`
- `System.runFinalization();`
- `Runtime.getRuntime().runFinalization();`

NOTE: Calling the preceding methods does not guarantee that GC will start performing and reclaiming the memory immediately. When all the heap memory is full, it will throw a java.lang.OutOfMemoryError error.

When GC fails to allocate the memory for new objects and is unable to reclaim the memory, JVM will generate and throw `java.lang.OutOfMemoryError`. This means heap is full and cannot extend memory further for new objects. There could be various reasons for this error, which we need to diagnose and determine. But mostly, this occurs due to insufficient heap memory, and to prevent this error, we need to increase the size of heap memory for JVM using Heap size parameters. We will discuss and investigate this to set various GC memory size later in this chapter.

Generations

Java Heap memory (Hotspot heap structure) is called **generations**. Generations are the logically divided spaces of heap memory to store the resources and objects based on their life or tenure. There are three generations in the heap memory - young generation, which is also called new generation, old generation, and permanent generation. Here is the figure of heap memory:

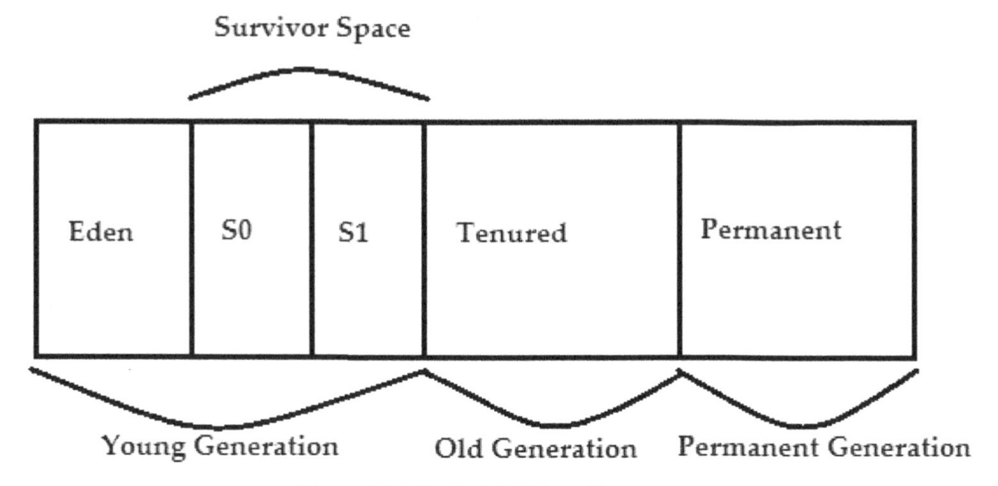

***Figure 16.1**: Logical division of heap memory*

The preceding figure shows the division of heap memory and how an object lives in the memory based on the use of object. Here generations - young generation, old generation, and permanent generation are three stacks in which an object lives according to the age of the object.

First, we have young generation that is split into three parts, an Eden, and two survivor space S0 and S1 that keep moving the object from one part to another by executing the Minor garbage collector.

Second, we have old generation, also known as tenured generation, that stores the objects, which does not get cleaned by Minor GC in young generation, and if a program or application still using that object, then that object will be moved to old generation of the heap memory. There is a threshold defined on the age of an object in young generation. Once that threshold age met, the object automatically moves from young to old generation. Major garbage collection runs on the old generation to clean the object and reclaim the memory.

The third one is permanent generation that holds the metadata of classes, objects, and members executed and loaded in the memory of running the program or application. It also holds Java library classes and methods. Full garbage collection runs on the permanent generation and clears the classes from memory when those classes and methods are no more required.

Types of garbage collection

There are three garbage collectors that get executed on respective generations of heap memory. Let's discuss and understand all three-garbage collectors (Minor, Major, and Full) with the help of examples:

- Minor GC: This runs on the new generation and is responsible for cleaning the dead objects and reclaiming the memory and keeps the memory available for young/new generation. Minor GC also moves the object from Eden to survivor spaces within the young generation, and later to old generation.
- Major GC: This runs on old generation of heap memory and responsible for cleaning the old/tenured heap space. When the old generation fills up, the JVM executes major garbage collection to reclaim the memory from dead objects. This also cleans the demon threads that are running in the background to keep the JVM up and running. Major garbage collection is slower in comparison to minor garbage collection and runs less frequently.
- Full GC: This is cleaning the entire heap memory, including young and tenured spaces.

These are three garbage collectors that run on their respective generations of heap memory and keeps our application active and running without any memory leakage issue or out of memory issue.

Finalize

Finalize is the method of garbage collection and is called by garbage collectors on objects to identify and check the references for that before reclaiming the memory. The **finalize()** method identifies the objects that do not have any references and pushes them in the garbage collection queue to reclaim the memory. The **finalize()** method will not send any live or active object for garbage collection.

We can explicitly call the **finalize()** method on objects, when we know that we are no longer going to use this object in the program and want to remove from memory. But again, it all depends on the GC, whether the memory will be reclaimed or not. We cannot guarantee that after calling the finalize method, memory of that object will be free and reclaimed. Calling the **finalize()** method explicitly may impact the performance of your application because of high CPU utilization. Here is the sample of overriding the garbage collection **finalize()** method:

```
@Override
protected void finalize() throws Throwable {
        super.finalize();
    }
```

It is always preferred to call the finalize using the super class, to remove the ambiguity, which is going to happen with sub-classes or inheritance. Thus, finalize will get executed when all the sub-classes of that super class get executed. To understand the role of super keyword, please refer to the inheritance section in *Chapter 10: Object Oriented Programming*, of this book.

Heap size

The heap size in any machine depends on the maximum address space per process. The following table shows the maximum per-process address values for various platforms:

Operating System	Maximum Address Space Per Process
Redhat Linux 32 bit	2 GB
Redhat Linux 64 bit	3 GB
Windows 98/2000/NT/Me/XP	2 GB
Solaris x86 (32 bit)	4 GB
Solaris 32 bit	4 GB
Solaris 64 bit	Terabytes

Table 16.1*: List of operating system and their maximum address space per process*

Heap Tuning

We can control the size of heap memory for any application or program while starting the program. Here are the parameters that we use to set the heap size and instruct the JVM to allocate the specified heap memory to an application:

- **-Xms<value>**: Xms define minimum heap size of memory
- **-Xmx<value>**: Xms define maximum heap size of memory
- **-XX:MinHeapFreeRatio=<minimumValue>**: The JVM grows or shrinks the heap at each GC to try to keep the proportion of free space to the living objects at each collection within a specific range. The minimum range is set as a percentage by the parameters **-XX:MinHeapFreeRatio=<MinValue>** within the total size bounded by **-Xms** and **-Xmx** parameters.
- **-XX:MaxHeapFreeRatio=<maximumValue>**: The JVM grows or shrinks the heap at each GC to try to keep the proportion of free space to the living objects at each collection within a specific range. The maximum range is set as a percentage by the parameters **-XX:MaxHeapFreeRatio=<MaxValue>** within the total size bounded by **-Xms** and **-Xmx** parameters.
- **-XX:NewRatio=<ratio>**: When the size of heap grows or shrinks, then JVM recalculates the size of young and old generation automatically. However, we can explicitly maintain the size of young and old generation by specifying NewRatio using the **-XX:NewRation** parameter. Let's understand this better: setting **-XX:NewRatio=3** means the ratio between the young and old generation is 3:1, and the total size of Eden and the two survivor spaces will be one fourth of the total heap.
- **-XX:NewSize=<size>**: This parameter is to set the minimum size for young generation.
- **-XX:MaxNewSize=<size>**: This parameter is to set the maximum size for young generation.
- **-XX:+AggressiveHeap**: This parameter examines the machine resources like size of memory and number of processors and tries to set various JVM parameters, which are best for long-running application and jobs.

We may set any of these parameters or as much as needed at the time of running a jar file or application. Here is an example of adding heap memory tuning parameters at the time of opening a **jar**:

```
java -jar javaCoreProject.jar -Xmx1024m -Xms3m -Xmn1m -XX:PermSize=20m
-XX:+UseSerialGC -XX:MaxPermSize=256M
```

java -jar is the command to open an application, which is built and packaged into **jar**. Here, we are opening the **javaCoreProject.jar** file with the JVM heap memory parameters. Here, the maximum memory is set to 1024mb using parameter **-Xmx1024m** and minimum **2mb**, next to that is **-Xms** and so on.

Conclusion

Memory management is the most pivotal things for any program or application to run the application on any system. JVM provides strong out of the box feature for memory management with the help of garbage collection. Due to this feature of JVM, a developer need not worry about the memory management while developing a Java application, since all these things are taken care by JVM itself.

We can explicitly specify and set the memory size for an application using tuning parameters and instruct and force JVM to trigger the GC. Minor, major, and full GC are the three GCs that help a Java application to reclaim the memory from unused or dead objects and make that available for new objects. Without GC, it will be challenging and difficult to decide when and what objects need to be removed from the memory and keep the memory space ready for new objects, and how to deal and handle the memory leaks.

Points to remember

- Garbage collector calls the finalize method for garbage collection. The finalize method is called on each object to identify the use or references of that object in Java.
- Heap memory is classified into three subsets, young or new generation, old generation, and permanent generation.
- Minor GC, major GC, and full GC are the three garbage collectors that run on young, old, and permanent generations, respectively.

Multiple choice questions

1. **Which of the following garbage collectors runs on old generation and removes the unused objects from old generation?**
    a. Full garbage collector
    b. Major garbage collector
    c. Half garbage collector
    d. Minor garbage collector
2. **Survivor spaces are part of which generation of heap memory?**
    a. Permanent generation
    b. Old generation
    c. Young generation
    d. Tenured generation

3. **Allocation of the memory for newly created object takes place in which heap memory?**
   a. Survivor space
   b. New generation
   c. Old generation
   d. Eden

Answers

1. b
2. c
3. d

Questions

1. What is the difference between Final, Finally, and Finalize?
2. Write the types of garbage collection.
3. Why JVM doesn't guarantee explicit execution of garbage collection? Write a short note.

Key terms

- **Heap**: Heap is a dynamic memory allocation that stores objects and variables. This is random access memory and resides in RAM of the computer.
- **Generation**: Generation is the logically divided part of the heap memory.
- **GC**: Garbage Collector or Garbage Collection
- **JVM**: Java virtual machine is the platform for Java on which Java program executes on any machine.

Glossary

- https://docs.oracle.com/cd/E19159-01/819-3681/abeik/index.html
- https://www.oracle.com/webfolder/technetwork/tutorials/obe/java/gc01/index.html

Index

T